OSPREY
ISHING

KU-196-804

Japanese Army in World War II

Conquest of the Pacific 1941–42

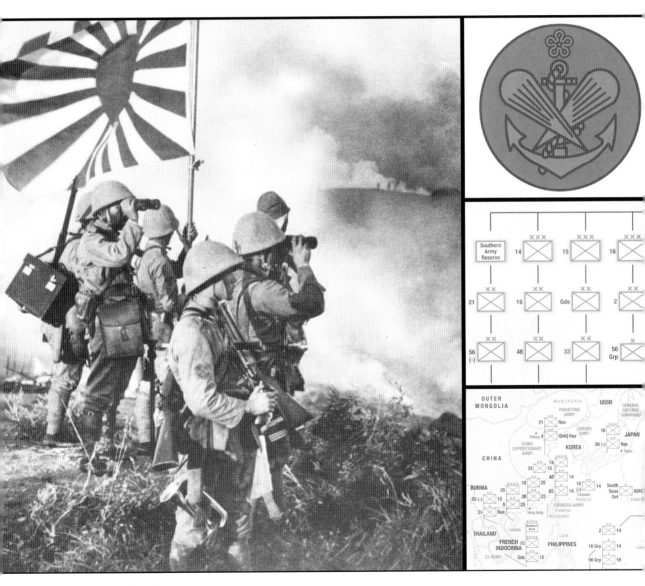

Gordon L Rottman · *Consultant editor Dr Duncan Anderson*

Series editors Marcus Cowper and Nikolai Bogdanovic

First published in Great Britain in 2005 by Osprey Publishing, Elms Court,
Chapel Way, Botley, Oxford OX2 9LP, United Kingdom.
Email: info@ospreypublishing.com

ISBN 1 84176 789 1

Editorial by Ilios Publishing, Oxford, UK (www.iliospublishing.com)
Design: Bounford.com, Royston, UK
Maps by Bounford.com, Royston, UK
Index by Alison Worthington
Originated by Grasmere Digital Imaging, Leeds, UK
Printed and bound by L-Rex Printing Company Ltd

05 06 07 08 09   10 9 8 7 6 5 4 3 2 1

FOR A CATALOGUE OF ALL BOOKS PUBLISHED BY OSPREY PLEASE CONTACT:

NORTH AMERICA
Osprey Direct, 2427 Bond Street, University Park, IL 60466, USA
E-mail: info@ospreydirectusa.com

ALL OTHER REGIONS
Osprey Direct UK, P.O. Box 140, Wellingborough,
Northants, NN8 2FA, UK
E-mail: info@ospreydirect.co.uk

www.ospreypublishing.com

Acknowledgements

Special thanks are due to Akira Takizawa, William Howard, and
Shigeyuki Mizuno.

Key to military symbols

xxxx Army	xxx Corps	xx Division	x Brigade	III Regiment	II Battalion	I Company/battery
●●● Platoon	●● Section	● Squad	Infantry	Cavalry	Artillery	Mountain
Airborne	Anti-tank	Armor/tank	Air Force	Anti-aircraft	Engineer	GD Grenade discharger
Headquarters	Infantry gun	LMG Light machine gun	MP Military Police	Maintenance	Mortar	Navy
Medical	Reconaissance	Signal	SNLF	Motorized transport		
V Veterinary	WPNS Weapons	Seaplane base	Airfield	Parachute landing site		
		Light machine gun	Grenade discharger			

Key to unit identification

Unit identifier — Parent unit — Commander

(+) with added elements   (-) less elements

Contents

Introduction

We, by the grace of Heaven, Emperor of Japan, seated on the Throne of a line unbroken for ages eternal, enjoin upon ye, Our loyal and brave subjects:

We hereby declare war on the United States of America and the British Empire. The men and officers of Our Army and Navy shall do their utmost in prosecuting the war, Our public servants of various departments shall perform faithfully and diligently their appointed tasks, and all other subjects of Ours shall pursue their respective duties; the entire nation with a united will shall mobilize their total strength so that nothing will miscarry in the attainment of Our war aims.

The Imperial Receipt, the 8th day of the 12th month of the 16th year of Showa, the Yamato year of 2601.

Japan (*Nippon*) viewed World War II, which it called the Greater East Asia War (*Dai Toa Senso Senkum*), as a series of interrelated wars. It had occupied parts of North China in 1931, and the war in China (*Shina Jihen*) began in earnest in 1937, in which Japan continued its creeping expansion. Conflict with the Soviet Union had occurred on the Siberian border in 1938–39 in Manchuria, or Manchuko, where a puppet state had been established by Japan in 1932. In July 1941, Japan occupied French Indochina in Southeast Asia. The Pacific War (*Taiheiyo Senso*) began at 02.15, December 8, 2601 Tokyo Time[1] ("X-Day") when the 2d Southern Expeditionary Fleet bombarded British forces at Kota Bharu, Malaya followed by amphibious landings. The first bomb detonated on Ford Island, Pearl Harbor, Hawaii at 03.45 Tokyo Time[1]. The same day, Japanese land, sea, and air forces also struck the northern Philippines, elsewhere in Malaya, Singapore, Hong Kong, Guam, Wake, and other Pacific islands.

The goal of the Greater East Asia War was to drive the armed forces of the Western colonial powers from the resource-rich Netherlands East Indies (NEI), the US-controlled Philippines, the Commonwealth possessions in the South Pacific, and British-controlled Malaya and Burma. A military operation of great magnitude would inflict a decisive defeat, resulting in the Western nations suing for peace, and allowing Japan to establish the Greater East Asia Co-prosperity Sphere (*Dai Toa Kyoei-Ken*). Ostensibly this was aimed at the mutual benefit and liberation of all Asians; in reality, its goal was Nippon's enrichment. Japan would colonize and maintain total control over East Asia exploiting its resources and establishing a security zone to protect it from the threat of Western influence.

This book covers the period from the beginning of the Greater East Asia War in December 1941 to the war's turning point in June 1942, the Battle of Midway. It covers operations in the Philippines, NEI, and South Pacific, but not those in China or Southeast Asia. Future planned volumes in the Battle Order series will cover Japanese operations in Southeast Asia 1941–45, the

---

1 Tokyo Time (Time Zone 21), which was used for all Japanese military and naval operations regardless of the local time zone, is indicated, for example, 03.45, as opposed to 0345. Dates west of the International Date Line are one day later than those to the east. Japan had adopted the Western solar, or Gregorian, calendar in 1873 to replace its lunar calendar, resulting in dates being advanced three to six weeks to bring days and months into common alignment. However, the new Japanese calendar began in the Western year of 660 BC (the founding of the Yamato State, predecessor of the Nippon Empire) resulting in 1941 being designated 2601.

South Pacific and New Guinea from 1942 to 1944, the 1944–45 defense of the Philippines, and Central and West Pacific operations from 1943 to 1945.

The genesis of the Imperial Japanese Army

Prior to the 1870s, Japan was a feudal society comprising over 200 semi-autonomous domains ruled by warlords of the *samurai* class. They owed their allegiance to the *Shogun*, the military ruler; the Emperor had been a mere figurehead since the late-12th century. For centuries Nippon existed in the form of a Western medieval state, and was subject to almost continuous civil war and rebellion.

Japan was opened to Western influence in the wake of US Commodore Matthew Parry's 1853 visit. Its exposure to modern technologies, especially with regard to weapons, resulted in a series of trade treaties with the US, Britain, Russia, France, and Holland. A popular slogan of the time was, "Eastern ethics, Western science," but others such as "Revere the Emperor, expel the barbarians" demonstrated the tensions that simmered beneath the surface.

Although Japan had been introduced to firearms in the mid-16th century, its *shogunate* armies still largely comprised sword-, spear-, and bow-and-arrow-armed *samurai* backed by peasant levies that owed allegiance to their particular clan. By 1860 muskets and cannons had come into wider use. In 1862 rifle units (*Shotai*) were formed with a mix of traditional and modern weapons, and the first distinctions were made between infantry, cavalry, and artillery branches. In 1866 the modern *Shotai*, manned with nationalist *samurai* who sought the restoration of the Emperor, defeated the *shogunate* army in battle. The Emperor was restored in 1868. Japan also seized control of Okinawa and the Ryukyu Islands in 1867.

The *Meiji* (Enlightened Rule) Era (1868–1912) saw major efforts to establish Japan's rightful place in the world and build a modern society. Not only were government and society considerably Westernized and modern industrialization efforts begun, but military advisors were also engaged, mostly from France but with others from Germany, Britain, and America. Officer training schools were established, although training was restricted to company level. The Imperial Guards (*Konoe*) were established in 1871 from the existing Imperial Bodyguard (*Goshinpei*) and armed and trained along Western lines. In February 1872 a separate army and navy were formally established. The army was called the *Nihongun* or *Kokugan*—Japan's or the Nation's army.

Conscription was instituted in 1873, with reserve service required after three years' active duty. Japan strove to establish a modern national army and followed the best European models, adapting them to its own requirements. In the wake of Prussia's defeat of France in 1870, Japan adopted German general staff and organizational principals, implementing its own General Staff in 1879. The General Staff College was opened in 1883. The Military Police (*Kempeitai*) was raised in 1881 and an Intendance Corps (administration and services) in 1888.

Tactically, Japan retained the concept of massed troop formations, much as per the old hand-to-hand battles, rather than the dispersed formations adopted in Europe. The day of the *samurai*, who lived on government stipends, was coming to an end though. They were offered a final lump sum, which was made compulsory in 1876; those who rejected it were forbidden to wear swords.

In 1885 the Emperor was given two means of directing military authority, *gunrei* and *gunsei*; it was a move that would have a major impact on how Japan made war in the future. *Gunrei* covered command, strategy, training, troop deployment, and discipline. This was executed through the Army Chief of Staff, and impacted on foreign affairs, by-passing the Prime Minister and Cabinet. *Gunsei* dictated military administration, the Army's size, armament, supplies, and conscription, and was executed through the War Minister.

In August 1894 Japan declared war on China to achieve its goal of gaining control of Korea, a longtime enemy. The stage had been set for such a move long before this in 1881, when Japan's security needs were defined to include the possibility of territorial expansion. In October 1894 the Japanese Army entered Manchuria in pursuit of a battered Chinese army driven from Korea. Japan's first modern war, and its first overseas expedition in centuries, won the Empire Korea, Formosa (Taiwan), the Pecadores Islands, and Liaotung Peninsula. In less than two decades Japan had progressed from a collection of clan armies led by feudal warlords wearing lacquered bamboo armor and kimonos and armed with swords and spears, to a unified, six-division, combined-arms force led by professional officers and armed with bolt-action repeating rifles and breech-loading artillery. The Chinese army defeated in the Sino-Japanese War was admittedly a poorly armed and led rabble, but Japan would prove her military prowess again soon after. Six more combined-arms divisions were authorized in 1896.

The construction of the Trans-Siberia Railroad increased Japanese fears of Russian expansion in Siberia. In 1900 the Boxer Rebellion broke out in China, and Japan provided almost a third of the troops for the eight-nation Peking relief expedition. As a result, Japan gained the right to station troops in China's international settlements, Peking and Tinsein, and the China Garrison Army was instituted. The 1904–05 Russo-Japanese War astounded the world with Japan soundly defeating Russia on both land and sea in a conflict over control of Manchuria. Although the Russians did not possess the most professional of armies, and the Japanese had their own shortcomings, the war saw the defeat of a long-established European power by an Oriental army still emerging from the medieval era.

In the Russo-Japanese War, the Japanese employed corps-level commands, designated "armies." It began the war with 13 divisions and ended with 17. Six more divisions were raised between 1905 and 1908 working toward the goal of 25 standing (*Jobi*) and 25 smaller reserve (*Kobi*) divisions to serve as replacements for the standing divisions. At the same time the Navy adopted its "eight-eight fleet" plan, comprising eight battleships and eight cruisers. By 1907 there were 19 active divisions. The war left Japan in control of Russia's Guandong (Kwantung) Peninsula leased territory[2], the Russian-built South Manchuria Railroad, and in a strong enough position to annex Korea outright in 1910. The Manchuria Garrison Force was established to secure the newly acquired territory. Japan was now in a perfect position to expand further into China in 1931.

The victory over Russia achieved far more than merely gaining territory and economic advantage for Japan; it gained the world's grudging respect. It also gave Japan a new self-confidence, increased its industrial capabilities, and placed the armed forces in a position of esteem. All of these factors would contribute to the Empire's increasing aspirations in acquiring territory and resources.

The *Taisho* (Great Righteousness) Era began with the accession of Emperor Yoshihito in 1912. With the armed forces still basking in the glories of the Russo-Japanese War, this era would soon see further expansion of the Army to garrison its territorial gains as well as the acquisition of new territories. It would end, however, with a reduction of its divisions by one fifth.

With the opening shots of World War I in 1914 Japan promptly took over the German colony in Tsingtao (Qingdao), China and the Kaiser's possessions in the Central Pacific, the Mariana, Caroline, and Marshall Islands, which would become springboards for Japan's future Pacific conquests. During World War I an additional two divisions were raised specifically to garrison Korea as the Chosen (Korea) Army, and a brigade was established on Formosa. In 1919 the Manchuria Garrison Force was redesignated the Kwantung Army. Japan began occupying

---

2 Kwantung is a small peninsula, on which Port Arthur is situated, jutting into the Yellow Sea between Korea and Tientsin, China. While bearing the designation of this small area, the Kwantung Army was eventually responsible for all of Manchuria and part of Inner Mongolia.

the Russian northern half of Sakhalin Island in 1920. This was a result of the otherwise muddled Siberian Expedition in which Japan supported Britain, America, and France to extract a Czechoslovak army that had been fighting with the Russians against Germany. It developed into an Allied effort to back the Whites fighting the Reds in which Japan refused to participate, except to consolidate its gains in the region. The Japanese Army now stood at 21 divisions.

While the Japanese studied World War I, its resources and its preconceived self-worth prevented it from absorbing many of its lessons, especially with regard to weaponry. It fully realized the value of light machine guns, trench mortars, and infantry guns and how these new weapons were critical to the infantry. They were adopted, but not until 1922. The Japanese still held that field artillery pieces were direct-fire weapons that belonged in the line alongside the infantry. To position artillery in the rear firing from protected positions was considered timid and would weaken the infantry's morale. They were slow in adopting artillery with high-trajectory fire and modern fire-control techniques. Another defect of artillery organization was that it lacked organic antiaircraft weapons. Likewise, tanks, aircraft, and poison gas were weapons embraced only reluctantly. They were not close-combat weapons, and were expensive as Japan lacked the industrial resources and technology to build them in quantity. Two air battalions were authorized in 1921, but had no fighters or bombers, only observation aircraft. Tank development was not begun until 1925 and would never catch up with the pace of Western advances.

In 1925 a major Army reduction was implemented. Four divisions (the 13th, 15th, 17th, and 18th) were deactivated with their 16 regiments—some 34,000 troops. This did have the benefit of allowing the fielding of two antiaircraft regiments and an experimental tank unit, adding much needed machine-gun and motor-transport units, expanding the two air battalions to regiments, and further development of radio communications. These divisions would later be reactivated when the Army began to expand. Additionally, 139 mostly non-divisional artillery companies were deactivated. Rather than a reduction this was labelled a consolidation permitting modernization, though many traditionalists opposed it. Enamored with the belief that military spirit could prevail over weapons, they branded modernization a false god and artillery was sacrificed to retain infantry strength.

The reason for it all: Japanese troops seize a Netherlands East Indies oilfield, the ultimate goal of the Southern Operations and the main reason for the conquest of the Southern Economic Zone. The troops are armed with 6.5mm Type 38 (1905) rifles and 6.5mm Type 11 (1922) LMGs.

The *Kokugan*, or national army, was redesignated *Dai Nippon Teikoku Rikugun* (or simply *Kogun*)—the Imperial Japanese Army (IJA). This, along with changing legislation, had wide-ranging effects on the psychological and legal authority of the Army, and its role. Whatever it did now, it did it for the Emperor.

The accession of Emperor Hirohito in 1926 saw the dawn of the *Sowa* (Enlightened Peace) Era and would soon see renewed efforts to dominate China. Between 1926 and 1939 well over a dozen new models of individual and infantry crew-served weapons, from pistols through machine guns to mortars and infantry guns, were adopted. New artillery, antiaircraft guns, and tanks were also fielded, but were inferior to contemporary Western designs and too few. Modern antitank weapons were essentially non-existent.

The 1930s saw Japan pursuing an aggressive policy in China initiating a series of "incidents," cumulating in the 1937 China Incident. (A Japanese "incident" could be any political-military event ranging from a minor skirmish to large-scale conflict, but short of declared war.) The Army incited much of this of its own accord, even ignoring orders to cease. Officers of the Kwantung Army initiated a plot to incite Chinese forces by dynamiting sections of the South Manchuria Railroad. Using this as an excuse, the Japanese occupied Mukden. While promising the League of Nations it would withdraw, another incident was initiated resulting in the invasion of the southern Manchuria provinces still in Chinese hands, ending in the rapid defeat of the defenders. In early-1932 the First Shanghai Incident was brought about, and the Japanese occupied the city to "protect" Japanese nationals. Further attacks were launched, more of Manchuria was occupied, and the puppet state of Manchukuo was established. Large numbers of Chinese guerrillas continued to fight in Manchuria, although the Japanese "anti-bandit" campaigns had been mostly successful by late-1934. Japan was condemned by the League of Nations in early-1932 for its aggression in China, which it ignored. This resulted in Japan tendering its two-year notification of its withdrawal from the League, which was finalized in 1935. On the heels of the condemnation, Japan occupied more of Inner Mongolia, incorporating it into Manchukuo. The Japanese position in China was now so strong that it forced the withdrawal of Chinese forces from Peking and Tiensin. A process of divisional triangularization began in 1936, with the elimination of a brigade headquarters and the withdrawal of an infantry regiment. This allowed the formation of additional divisions. The Kwantung Army continued small-scale operations throughout northern China into 1937. On July 7, 1937 the Japanese engineered the Marco Polo Bridge Incident outside of Peking, leading to all-out war with China known as the China Incident. This was seen as a chance to neutralize the Chinese as a threat to the Japanese southern flank. It would then allow Japan to face the "real" enemy, the Soviets threatening Manchuria. The policy overall was known as the "Strike North."

Over 180,000 Japanese troops died in China and over 400,000 were taken sick or wounded—only a few years prior to the beginning of the Pacific War. With 23 divisions fighting the Chinese, nine were prepared to fight the Soviets. Fighting broke out on the Siberian border with the USSR in 1938 and 1939 resulting in embarrassing Japanese defeats in the long awaited confrontation. French Indochina was occupied in 1941 through "agreement" with the colonial government after the fall of France. A million troops were mobilized during 1940. The feasibility of invading the south was studied and what were termed "Strike South" command exercises were conducted. Through all this Japan significantly increased its divisions, air service, and other units to bring the IJA to 51 divisions, 59 brigade equivalents, and 151 air battalions on the eve of the Greater East Asia War. Of these divisions nine had been organized in 1940 and one in 1941.

Table 1: disposition of Imperial Japanese Army forces, December 1, 1941 (exclusive of Southern Operations Forces)

Home Islands

General Defense Command

    Eastern District Army

        52d Division

        2d, 3d, 51st, 57th Depot divisions

    Central District Army

        53d, 54th divisions

        4th, 5th, 55th Depot divisions

    Western District Army

        6th, 56th Depot divisions

    Northern District Army

        7th Division

        Karafuto Mixed Brigade

    1st Air Group (nine air battalions)

4th Division (IGHQ Reserve)

Manchuria

Kwantung Army

    10th, 28th, 29th divisions

    23d Tank Regiment

    3d Army

        9th, 12th divisions

        1st Tank Group

    4th Army

        1st, 14th, 57th divisions

    5th Army

        11th, 24th divisions

        2d Tank Group

    6th Army

        23d Division

    20th Army

        8th, 25th divisions

        Four brigades

    Manchuria Defense Command

        Five brigades

    Manchuria Air Brigade (21 air battalions)

    2d Air Group (35 air battalions)

North China

China Expeditionary Army

    North China Area Army

        27th, 35th, 110th divisions

            1st, 7th, 8th IMBs

(continued on page 10)

	15th Tank Regiment	
1st Army		
	36th, 37th, 41st divisions	
	3d, 4th, 9th, 16th IMBs	
12th Army		
	17th, 32d divisions	
	5th, 6th IMBs	
Mongolia Garrison Army		
	26th Division	
	Mongolia Cavalry Group	
	2d IMB	
11th Army		
	3d, 6th, 13th, 34th, 39th, 40th divisions	
	14th, 18th IMBs	
13th Army		
	15th, 22d, 116th divisions	
	11th, 12th, 13th, 17th, 20th IMBs	
23d Army		
	38th, 51st, 104th divisions	
	19th IMB	
1st Air Brigade (16 air battalions)		
Korea		
Chosen Army		
	19th, 20th divisions	
Formosa		
Formosa Army (combat units detached to Southern Army)		

The outbreak of the Pacific War, 1941

A detailed exposé of Japan's reasons for going to war with America, Great Britain[3], and the Netherlands is beyond the scope of this book. In brief, the League of Nations condemned Japan's increasingly brutal, but bogged down, war of aggression in China. Economic embargos were implemented by the Pacific colonial powers as a result, especially forbidding the exportation of oil and other resources to Japan, resources it did not possess. Verging on a collapse of its war effort and national economy, Japan was forced to secure a vast region of Southeast Asia and the South Pacific in order to control the natural resources it required for its survival. At the same time it would establish a security zone in which to exploit and transport these resources to the Home Islands and between the areas it controlled. Japan realized an extended war was possible. It was essential that the "Southern Resource Area" be secured and exploited as quickly as possible in order to wage a protracted war. She possessed liquid fuel stockpiles adequate for less than two years of war. A National Defense Zone would be established through Burma down though the NEI (Sumatra, Java, Timor), Western New Guinea, the Caroline and Marshall Islands (Japanese Mandated Territory), anchored on the remote Wake Island in the north.

---

3 Japan made little distinction between Britain, Australia, and New Zealand and seldom referred to the British Commonwealth. In Japan's eyes Britain was a colonial power and the Commonwealth members mere colonies of a Western power. Japan simply used "Britain" or "the British" as collective terms.

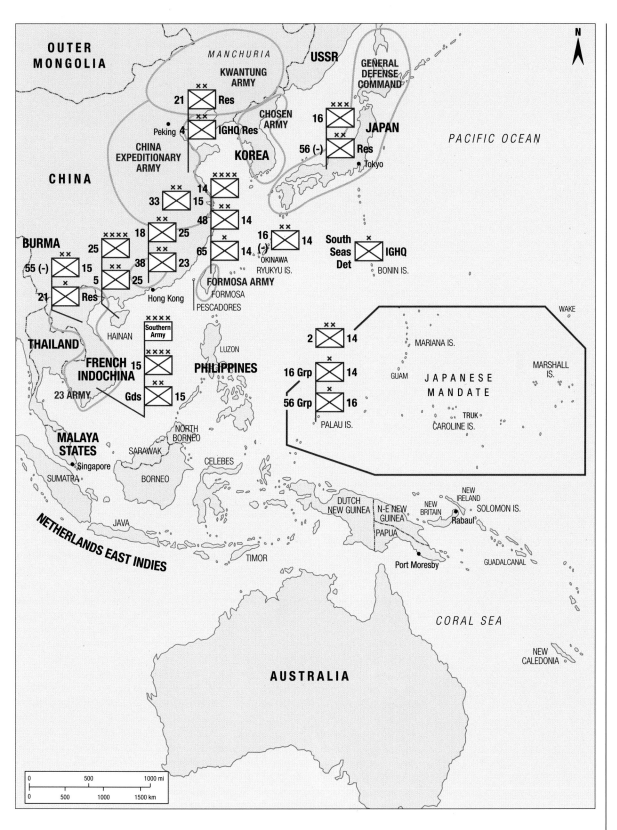

The Southern Army's pre-invasion deployment, December 1941. Only units assigned to Southern Army are indicated.

Eastern New Guinea would be secured as well as the Gilbert and Solomon Islands as a buffer zone. The conquered Southeast Asia areas of the NEI, British Borneo, and the Philippines would be defended by the IJA, and naval and air forces of the Combined Fleet would engage any attacking fleets in what was envisioned as a Jutland-like decisive engagement. The IJN was also responsible for the defense of most of New Guinea, the Solomons, Carolines, Marshalls, and Gilberts. It was hoped that the Allies, after repeated humiliating defeats, would sue for peace and leave the Empire of the Sun to itself within its Greater East Asia Co-prosperity Sphere.

With no diplomatic solution believed obtainable, Japan committed itself to war with the Western colonial powers on November 5, 1941. Initial preparations for "Z Operation" had long been underway; the Pearl Harbor attack had been proposed in January 1941 and IJA units had begun training in August, but it was in the early days of November that the final orders were issued. Intelligence collection had been underway for years. The objectives were the destruction of the major US and Commonwealth fleet units and the seizure of the Philippines, NEI, Malaya, Thailand, Southern Burma, Hong Kong, Singapore, and Commonwealth possessions in the South Pacific. The American territory of Guam, within the Japanese Mandated Territory, was also a key objective.

Since the mid-1920s the IJA had allotted three divisions to seize Luzon and one for Guam. America though was not considered the main enemy. That distinction fell to the USSR. Bogged down in a seemingly endless war in China, Japan hoped to secure the Southern Resource Zone within five months and then redeploy half of the forces to Manchuria. They would be prepared by the spring of 1943 for the USSR to collapse under the German invasion or pull most of its 20 divisions out of Siberia to face the Germans. The fact that France and the Netherlands had been occupied by Germany, and that Britain looked likely to follow soon, spurred the Japanese on. America was viewed as weak because its individualism and liberalism would prevent it from fighting a lengthy war. By August 1941 Japan had temporarily abandoned the idea of attacking the USSR and began to focus attention to the "Strike South" concept.

The order assigning forces to the Southern Army was issued on November 6 and objectives assigned to specific units on the 20th. The Combined Fleet issued its first orders and assignments on November 5 and "X-Day," the start of hostilities, was designated as December 8. This was fixed on December 2, as the Pearl Harbor Task Force was en route to its target, to commence at approximately 05.30 on December 8 (Tokyo Time). A high degree of cooperation would be required between the IJA and Imperial Japanese Navy (IJN). The Army–Navy Central Agreement was signed on November 10 by the commanders-in-chief of the Southern Army and Combined Fleet.

Combat mission

The Southern Army (often incorrectly identified as "Southern Area Army") was established on November 6, 1941 to control all IJA units assigned to the Southern Operations. The command was headquartered in Saigon, French Indochina under Gen. Count Terauchi Hisaichi (also listed as Juichi). The plan was certainly ambitious. The seizure of all of Southeast Asia, the NEI, the Philippines, and regions of the South Pacific would be accomplished by only 11 infantry divisions, four brigade-size forces, and 700 IJA aircraft—400,000 troops in total. This area stretched across five time zones and was larger than the Continental United States. Japan was counting on surprise, and the relatively unprepared and weak forces fielded by the colonial powers. Its own resources would be stretched to the limit with transport shipping pulling double duty to move troops. The units initially assigned to the Philippines, Hong Kong, Malaya, and Guam would be tasked with follow-on missions and then serve as occupation troops or conduct further combat operations. Almost half of the IJA's 1,500 combat aircraft would be required and the best air units were taken from other commands for assignment to the 3d and 5th Air Groups.

In December 1941 Japan possessed 51 divisions supplemented by 59 brigade-equivalents[4], but many of these were non-deployable being garrison and line-of-communications security forces in China. Twenty-eight divisions were in China with most engaged in combat or occupation duty. Another 13 were in Manchuria and Korea to protect the Empire's northern frontier with the USSR. Two of the five divisions remaining in the Home Islands were newly raised and partly trained. The exceptions were the 2d committed to the Southern Operations, the 4th as the IGHQ Reserve, and the 7th tied down protecting northern Japan from the USSR. There were also 10 brigades in Japan and nine depot divisions training replacements.

The 11 divisions and other forces assigned to the Southern Army were drawn from a number of sources and scattered throughout the Empire when the Southern Army was organized. Five divisions came from the Home Islands, five from China, and one from Formosa.

The 14th Army was designated the Philippines Attack Force with its headquarters and army troops, 48th Division, and 65th Brigade on Formosa while the 16th Division was on Amami Shima in the Ryukyu Islands. Other small elements were in the Palaus and Pescadores. The 5th Air Group (20 air battalions) from Manchuria was deployed to Formosa for the Philippines operation with two fighter, two light-bomber, and one heavy-bomber regiments plus a reconnaissance unit. It was estimated the operation would require approximately 50 days. At the end of this phase part of 14th Army forces would be reassigned to complete the more critical NEI operation. The 4th Division, the IGHQ Reserve in Japan, would be committed to the Philippines later.

The Burma Attack Force, which would first secure Thailand, was built around the 15th Army in Indochina with the headquarters and a detachment of the 55th Division in the south along with the Guards Division (temporarily detached from 25th Army). The 55th Division (less elements) was in the north and the follow-on 33d Division still in Central China. Burma operations would subsequently be reinforced from units released from other areas. Its completion was forecast to be within 100 days.

---

4 Independent mixed brigades, independent infantry brigades, independent infantry groups, independent mixed regiments, independent infantry regiments, and independent garrison units.

The East Indies Attack Force's 16th Army headquarters was in Japan with the 2d Division while the 56th Infantry Group was forward-deployed in the Palaus. The operation was allotted approximately 150 days to complete—an almost leisurely pace. Other units would later be assigned to complete the operation.

The 25th Army, the Malaya Attack Force, was widely scattered with its headquarters and 5th Division on Hainan Island off the South China coast, 18th Division at Canton, China, and the army troops on Formosa. Besides Malaya, the 25th Army would also seize Sumatra, Borneo, and Celebes in the NEI. The 38th Division, the Hong Kong Attack Force, was under the control of the 23d Army under Lt Gen Sakai Takashi in Canton. It was allotted 10 days to complete its mission. The 3d Air Group (48 air battalions) detached from the China Expeditionary Army would support the Malaya invasion. Based in South China and northern Indochina, it consisted of five fighter, four light-bomber, four heavy-bomber, and two reconnaissance regiments.

The South Seas Detachment was built around the 55th Infantry Group of the 55th Division and located in the Bonin Islands. It was assigned to the Guam Occupation Force, an IJN command under the direct control of the IGHQ. It would later seize New Britain. The Southern Army Reserves were the 21st Division in North China and the 56th Division (less elements) in Japan and they too would be committed in the later stages of the Southern Operations. The 21st Independent Mixed Brigade was in Indochina, but would not be committed to Malaya until later. Southern Army service and support units were largely drawn from the Kwantung Army.

Special Naval Landing Force (SNLF)[5] units were assigned to all operations to secure specific objectives, some independent of the IJA and others in joint operations. Only naval forces would secure the Gilberts and Solomons. Extensive participation by land-based Navy Air Service (NAS) units of the Formosa-based 11th Air Fleet (21st and 23d Air flotillas, 444 aircraft) would be seen in the Philippines, Malaya, and NEI as well as carrier aircraft. The Navy had longer range goals than the Army. Rabaul on New Britain would be a base from which to continue the conquest. The Army thought of Rabaul only as an out guard for the naval base at Truk in the Carolines. The Navy desired to seize Port Moresby in May, Midway and the western Aleutian Islands in June, hoping for a decisive engagement with the US Pacific Fleet, New Caledonia in July, and Fiji and Samoa in August. The IJN's future plans were even more ambitious with proposals to invade Hawaii, northern Australia, and Ceylon off India.

The plan further allowed for the reduction to seven divisions in the south and their redeployment to Manchuria to prepare for war with the USSR. Even longer range planning was conducted to prepare for a 10-year war with the USSR and America. Some 100 divisions and 1,000 air battalions were forecast for 1950.

Southern Operations forces

The 14th, 15th, and 16th armies had been organized specifically for the Southern Operations. The 25th Army had previously operated in China. Army troops varied greatly, but usually included a signal regiment, one or more tank regiments, several artillery regiments and independent battalions, field AA battalions and companies, mortar battalions, specialized engineer regiments and smaller units, construction units, transport units, shipping engineer and debarkation units, hospitals, field motor transport and ordnance depots, and small service units.

Japanese troops take down the Stars and Stripes on Corregidor, May 6, 1942. The Japanese were reported to have lost 900 dead and 3,000 wounded in the assault, but this appears to be an inflated figure as fewer troops than this participated. The flagpole was removed from a captured Spanish ship in 1898. The US flag was raised again here when the island was recaptured on March 2, 1945 and still remains on the island today.

---

5 An SNLF (Tokubetsu Rikusentai) was the size of a large battalion. The naval base at which they were raised prefixed their designations. It is incorrect to refer to them as "Imperial Marines."

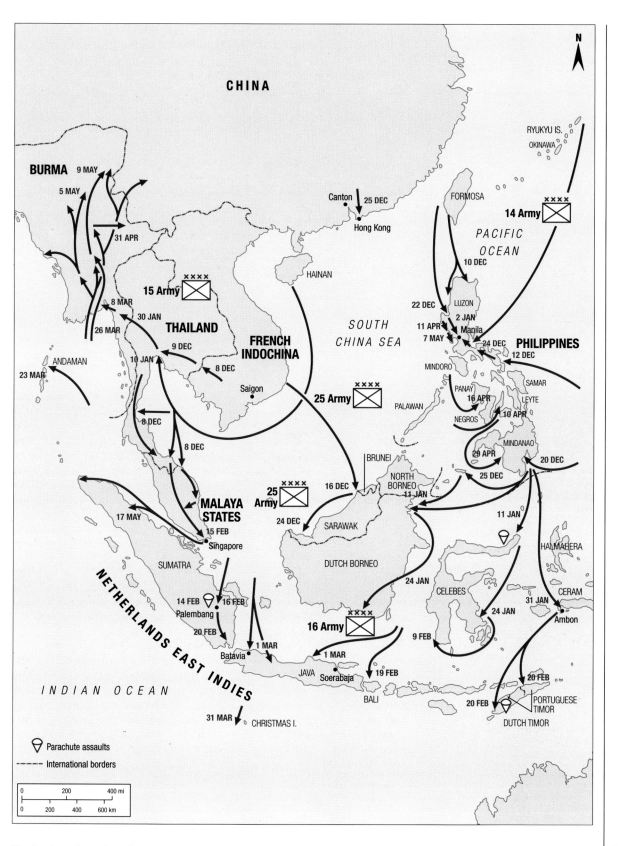

The Southern Operations plan.

Table 2: Southern Operations initial forces

Southern Army, Gen Count Terauchi Hisaichi	
21st, 56th (-) divisions	**Southern Army Reserve**
21st Independent Mixed Brigade	
4th Independent Mixed Regiment	
14th Army, LtGen Homma Masaharu	**Philippines Attack Force**
16th, 48th divisions	
65th Brigade	
4th, 7th Tank regiments	
5th Air Group LtGen Obata Hideyoshi	
15th Army, LtGen Iida Shojiro	**Burma Attack Force**
Guards, 33d, 55th (-) divisions	
2d Tank Regiment	
16th Army, LtGen Imamura Hitoshi	**East Indies Attack Force**
2d Division	
35th Infantry Group	
56th Infantry Group	
25th Army, LtGen Yamashita Tomoyuki	**Malaya Attack Force**
5th, 18th (-) divisions	
1st, 6th, 14th Tank regts (3d Tank Group)	
3d Air Group LtGen Sugawara Michita	
38th Division (23d Army-control)	**Hong Kong Attack Force**
South Seas Detachment (IGHQ-control)	**Guam Occupation Force**

Note: component units of these divisions and brigades are provided in the Unit Organization chapter.

21st Division	This division was activated at Kanazawa, Japan in July 1938 and deployed to China before the year's end. In November 1941 it moved to Indochina. The 21st Infantry Group and 62d Infantry landed on Luzon in February 1942 to complete operations there. They returned to Indochina in early-1943 where it remained. Commander: LtGen Tanaka Hisaichi.
56th Division	This was a new division raised in August 1940 in Kurume, Japan. Its 56th Infantry Group landed on Mindanao, Philippines in December 1941 and later fought on Java. The division itself served in Burma from March 1942 where it remained through the war. Commander: LtGen Matsuyama Yuzo.
21st Independent Mixed Brigade	Organized in January 1941 from the 170th Infantry, 104th Division at Osaka, Japan. It served as an occupation force in Indochina at the beginning of 1942 and was then sent to Malaya, and later fought at Rabaul. Part of the brigade was destroyed on New Guinea after landing in December. II/170 was stationed on Wake and absorbed into 13th Independent Infantry Regiment. The brigade was deactivated in July 1943. Commander: MajGen Yamagata Ylkao.
16th Division	Activated in Kyoto, Japan in 1905 because of the Russo-Japanese War, in which it did not fight. It was deployed to Manchuria in 1934, returning to Japan in 1936. It fought in North China from 1937 to 1939 and then again returned to Japan where it was triangularized in 1941. It landed on Luzon in December 1941. It remained there until transferred to Leyte in April 1944 where it was destroyed. Commander: LtGen Morioka Susumu.
48th Division	Organized on Formosa in late-1940 from the Formosa Mixed Brigade and the 47th Infantry dropped from the 6th Division, which had also fought in China. The brigade had fought in China from 1937 to 1940, soon after it had been raised. It fought on Luzon from December 1941 until deployed to Java in January 1942 to complete operations there. It was then transferred to Timor in late-1942, where it remained. Commander: LtGen Tsuchihashi Yuitsu.

 (continued on page 17)

65th Brigade	This brigade was raised at Hiroshima, Japan in early-1941 from the 65th Independent Infantry Group. It was sent to Formosa and then landed on Luzon in December 1941. It fought there and remained on the island until December 1942 when one regiment and the HQ were sent to Rabaul and the other regiments elsewhere. The brigade was dissolved in late-1943 after its units were absorbed into others. Commander: MajGen Naka Akira.
Guards Division *(Konoe Shidan)*	Activated in 1867 in Tokyo, it grew in size over the years. Its 2d Guards Brigade and two regiments were sent to China in 1940 to experience their first combat. In 1941 the 1st Guards Brigade and its units were detached and reorganized as the Guards Mixed Brigade. The 2d Brigade units in China became the new Guards Division with augmentation by the 5th Guards Infantry. In mid-1941 the division went to Indochina then Thailand and Malaya. In March 1942 is was deployed to Sumatra, and in June 1943 was re-designated the 2d Guards Division when the Mixed Guards Brigade in Japan became the 1st Guards Division. Commander: LtGen Muto Akira.
33d Division	Organized in March 1939 at Sendai, Japan and sent to China the following month where it completed training. It fought in Central China until departing for Thailand in December 1941. By March 1942 it was fighting in Burma, where it remained. Commander: LtGen Sakurai Shozo.
55th Division	Activated in August 1940 at Zentsuji, Japan. The Division (less elements) arrived in Indochina in December 1941 and went into Burma. Its 55th Infantry Group and 144th Infantry formed the South Seas Detachment, which secured Guam and Rabaul. Turned back from Port Moresby during the Battle of the Coral Sea, it was later landed at Buna, and was destroyed. It was rebuilt and rejoined the division in Burma in 1943 where it ended the war. Commander: LtGen Takeuchi Yiroshi.
2d Division	Raised in 1870, it fought in the Sino-Japanese and Russo-Japanese wars. It deployed to Manchuria in the 1930s and was soon engaged in North China; it then fought the Soviets in Manchuria in 1939. It returned to Japan in 1940, and again departed in January 1942 to arrive on Java in March, where it helped complete the operation. It was sent to Rabaul, later destroyed on Guadalcanal, rebuilt at Rabaul, and spent the rest of the war in Southeast Asia. Commander: LtGen Maruyama Masao.
5th Division	Organized in 1873, it remained a square division at the beginning of the war and was partly motorized as well as amphibious trained. It fought in the Sino-Japanese and Russo-Japanese wars. It deployed to China in 1937, fighting there until September 1940 when it went to Indochina. It conducted brief operations in China and then moved to Hainan Island off South China before landing in Thailand. From late-1942 it occupied and garrisoned various small islands in the NEI. The 41st Infantry was detached and fought on Panay and Mindanao in the Philippines and then on New Guinea, where it was partly destroyed. It was reassigned to the 30th Division. Commander: LtGen Matsui Takuro.
18th Division	Activated in 1905 at Kurume, Japan, it was deactivated in 1925 as part of the IJA's reduction. It was reactivated in September 1937 as a square division. It moved to China in November to complete its training, where it saw much action until late-1941. It landed in Malaya in December and subsequently fought in Burma where it remained. Its 35th Infantry Brigade and 124th Infantry were detached and served on Borneo, then Mindanao, and finally Guadalcanal where it was largely destroyed. It was rebuilt on Truk and sent to Burma, where it was reassigned to the 31st Division. Commander: LtGen Mutaguchi Renya.
38th Division	Raised at Nagoya, Japan in February 1939, it deployed to China in December. It soon seized Hong Kong. From there it sent regiments to Java, Sumatra, Timor, and other NEI islands. It assembled on Java in late-1942 and moved to Rabaul. Much of the division was lost on Guadalcanal. It was rebuilt at Rabaul, where it remained understrength. Commander: LtGen Sano Tadayoshi.
4th Division	Organized in 1870, it fought in the Sino-Japanese and Russo-Japanese wars. It deployed to Manchuria in 1937 and fought in China until November 1941. It landed on Luzon in February 1942 and concluded the operation. It returned to Japan in June where it remained until September 1943 when it was sent to garrison Sumatra. Some detached battalions fought in Burma. The division moved to Thailand in April 1945. Commander: LtGen Kitano Kenzo.

Doctrine

SNLF troops shine flashlights on an American flag to indicate to aircraft that they have captured Agaña, Guam. This drawing from the 50th Anniversary booklet shows the troops wearing rising sun armbands, a detail which has not been verified.

The IJA developed its tactical doctrine over the 40-year period prior to the outbreak of World War II by studying and adopting aspects of Western armies that best suited its needs. No one army served as a pure model though, and aspects of doctrine would be modified to fit their traditional concepts. Japanese combat experience during the 40-year period in question was more diverse than often thought. They fought Chinese forces of varying quality, ranging from warlord-led gangs, through guerrillas, to professionally led, well-organized forces of substantial size and quality. They also fought well-trained, skillfully led, and better-equipped Soviet forces. The IJA also gained vast experience of fighting in different terrain, climate, and operational conditions. These included the barren plains of Siberia against armored and mechanized forces; the forests, plains, rugged hills and mountains of northern and central China; and in cities and villages. The climate extremes ranged from biting cold to desert heat, from torrential rain to dust storms. Many of the areas fought in lacked developed road systems and railroads.

Contrary to popular early-war perception, the Japanese were not trained for jungle warfare nor were they "natural" jungle fighters. Japan had no place in which to conduct such training and most troops were farmers, fisherman, and urban workers. Most units that fought in the Pacific and Southeast Asia deployed directly from the chilly fall climates of China, Manchuria, or Japan. What their previous experience did provide was the ability to operate in varied terrain and climate conditions against enemy forces of equally varied quality and capabilities. Their own self-inflicted austere field conditions were a major factor and prepared them well. With such experience behind them the Japanese were able to study the conditions of the expected areas of operation and adapt their tactics, equipment levels, task organization, and logistics accordingly. They were not always successful in this, for example on New Guinea, where they greatly underestimated the conditions. Their equipment was already comparatively light and much of it designed to be man- or animal-packed. Their logistics tail was less burdensome than any Western army's, although this meant it was fragile and easily disrupted.

Offensive operations

Japanese tactical doctrine focused on attack, surprise, rapid movement, commanders operating well forward, and relatively simple plans. Offensive actions were the norm. In the 1928 edition of *Tosui Koryo* (*Principles of Strategic Command*), the words defense, retreat, and surrender were expunged, as they were considered

The Japanese forces were fairly well equipped with light bridging and bridge-repair *matériel*. They recognized the necessity of maintaining the speed of offensive operations through difficult terrain.

detrimental to morale and the military spirit. The Japanese found defensive actions to be abhorrent. If a Japanese officer were confronted with an unexpected, unusual, or complicated situation in battle, he would find a way to attack. An attack would be executed at unexpected times and places, along unanticipated routes and often with force ratios that Western armies would not have used, all of which would increase the element of surprise. Rapid movement, besides benefiting tactical and operational maneuver, also increased this, and was achieved by forced marches. The Spartan equipment and austere logistics allowed troops to move at comparatively high speed over terrain that Western armies would consider difficult for large forces.

Seishin—strength of will

The IJA also placed complete faith in seishin, its strength of will and spirit over the *matériel* superiority of its enemies. While Western thought tended to dismiss such intangible aspects, often pointing to several Japanese disasters brought about by misplaced faith in this, it was nonetheless an influencing factor, with certain limitations. Belief in this was so strong and the Japanese soldier so hardened to field conditions that *seishin* certainly contributed to many of the feats of endurance that astounded Western opponents. Regardless of the class system and the separation between officers and men, Japanese officers willingly shared the perils of combat with their troops. Officers led from the front, and at much higher echelons than was common among their Western counterparts. Command posts were often located further forward than Western practice. Officers were required to be as physically and mentally tough as their men. The Japanese counterattack in the first days of the 1944 Guam landing is a fitting example of this. About 95 percent of the attacking units' officers were killed including most company and battalion commanders, along with the commanders of the attacking brigade and two regiments. The first experiences that US troops encountered of Japanese troops fighting to the death, on Tulagi and Gavutu-Tanabogo Islands on August 7, 1942, came as a shock. Some 900 SNLF, construction, and air service troops defended these three tiny islands across The Slot from Guadalcanal. About 70 escaped by swimming to larger Florida Island, 23 prisoners were taken, and the rest died fighting. The three Marine assault battalions lost 145 dead and 194 wounded. It was a sobering experience and would prove to be the norm. An earlier instance of this, when a Japanese battalion landed behind US–Filipino lines on Bataan in January 1942, was not commonly known of by American troops reconquering the Pacific. The trapped battalion of 900 men fought to the death without a single man surrendering.

The Japanese often violated certain fundamental principles of doctrine. Their biggest failure was to underestimate the enemy, especially following an initial success. This was a combination of overconfidence, arrogance, and over-reliance on the strength of spirit. The expectation was that the enemy would do as Japanese plans had predicted; the Japanese themselves were often too inflexible to adapt to unanticipated enemy reactions. Often, another serious flaw was the lack of reconnaissance. While detailed reconnaissance was established doctrine, in practice, with the rush to attack, it was often neglected or based on unrealistic estimates, with dire consequences. Another area in which there were severe shortfalls was logistics. Many staff officers felt logistical concerns were beneath them and focused on offensive planning. The early operations against unprepared enemy forces were successful in spite of marginal logistics support, reinforcing this belief.

Complete annihilation of the enemy was the goal sought in most operations. Allowing the enemy to escape to fight again was unacceptable. This of course resulted in the surrender of large numbers of Allied prisoners, who did not fight to the death as the Japanese did and who could not be easily disposed of, as the Chinese were. The conquering of colonial territories also meant that large numbers of Western civilians were interned, for which the Japanese were totally unprepared. The treatment of prisoners and internees varied greatly depending on

A well-known photo of victorious 61st Infantry troops on Corregidor—*Tenno Heiha! Banzai!* (Long Live the Emperor! Hurrah!')

local commanders. There was little guidance on such matters. This was also often the case with matters such as the disposition of captured equipment and installations, the treatment of local populations, local security arrangements, and the establishment of effective defenses in occupied territories.

Amphibious operations

The IJA's amphibious doctrine was well developed long before the start of the Greater East Asia War, a process that had begun in the 1920s. Japan was one of the first countries to recognize its importance, and a great deal of experience had been gained during the conflict in China where joint-landing operations were commonly conducted by the IJA and IJN. Doctrinal development did not progress much after the mid-1930s though. It remained focused on China and the USSR, and was not as advanced as is often stated: operations were generally conducted on a smaller scale and were less robust than later Allied operations. However, the IJA did possess adequate landing craft and specialized shipping engineer units to support such operations.

While the IJA took the lead in amphibious doctrine and landing craft design, the latter influencing early Allied designs, the IJN also developed doctrine. Regardless of the IJA's and IJN's much touted rivalry, a joint doctrine was created and the early-war landings were successfully accomplished. This joint doctrine called for thorough planning; reconnaissance of the landing areas; a sequence of assault unit, reserve and support landings; rehearsals; naval gunfire and air support; and deception procedures. The cross-loading of transports was critical, for example, so that the loss of any one ship would not mean the loss of an entire artillery unit. Supplies and equipment were loaded to allow their debarkation according to the priority of need.

The naval force conducting the landing operation, usually designated the "occupation force," was responsible for the overall operation. The escort force

Maizuru 2d SNLF landing sites: Lae, Huon Gulf, northeast New Guinea, March 8, 1942.

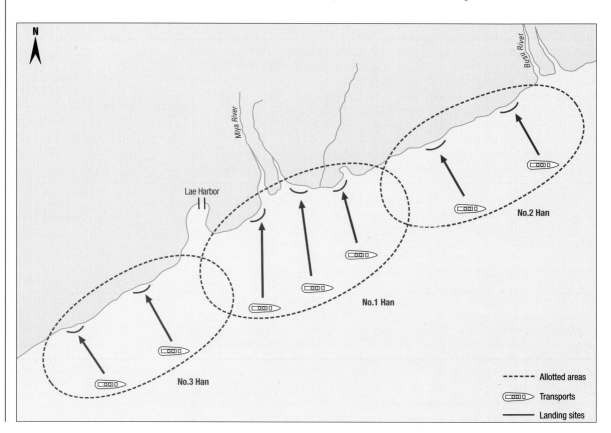

commander, superior to the convoy commander, provided fire and air support. The convoy commander was responsible for the embarkation, movement, and debarkation of the landing force. The Army transport officer commanded the shipping engineers and other troops supporting the debarkation.

To maintain surprise, reconnaissance elements were seldom landed. Reconnaissance was usually conducted by surveillance from the sea and air. Often only general landing sites were selected in advance and precise sites designated after reconnaissance and assessment of the enemy situation. Transport anchorages and landing sites were often selected by running fast patrol boats through the inshore area. Every effort was made to land unopposed. There were instances when the Japanese encountered fire from the shore, and as a result the landing forces simply shifted to another site; after landing, they then attempted to encircle the defenders from the rear. The Japanese conducted very few opposed landings and nothing comparable to those undertaken by the US, such as Tarawa, Saipan, and Peleliu. In most instances the only resistance encountered came from artillery fire and air attack. However, a major goal of Japanese landing operations was to gain local sea and air superiority.

The actual landing was almost always conducted in darkness, just before dawn or even earlier (most Allied landings were conducted well after dawn). This led to control problems and confusion on the beach, factors outweighed by increased surprise and protection of the landing force from artillery and air attack. There were several examples of the defenders expecting daylight landings, only to find themselves overrun before dawn. If a daylight landing were required, ship-generated smoke would blind defenders and screen the approaching landing craft. Another significant difference between Japanese and Allied landings was that the Japanese would not land units on adjoining beaches; instead, they would land on sites often widely separated from each other. For example, four forces were landed on Guam with anything from five to 20 miles separating them. On some

The Port Moresby invasion plan, May 9, 1942. Even in an amphibious assault, the doctrine of flanking and enveloping the enemy can be seen.

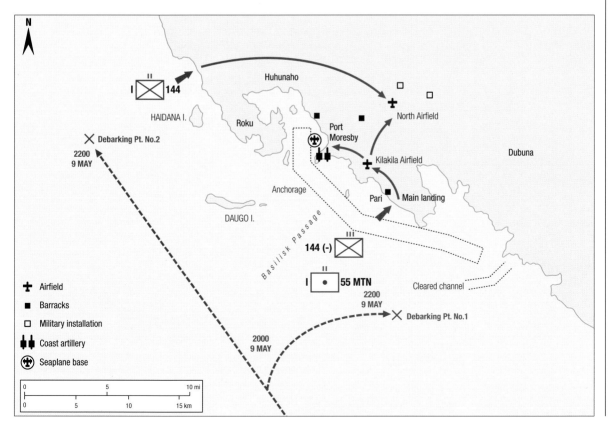

The 49ft Type A landing barge, or *Daisatsu*, was the most commonly used model by the IJA. It was powered by a 6-cylinder gasoline or diesel engine, giving it a top speed of 8–10 knots. It might be armed with two LMGs, and could carry 100–120 men, or 10 horses, or an artillery piece, or a light tank, or a light truck. There was also a longer-ranged IJN version of the Type A.

of the larger Philippine islands three or four forces were landed separated by even greater distances. Regimental and divisional landings were often conducted by landing two or three units abreast, the distance separating them depending on suitable landing sites, terrain, enemy deployment, road networks, and the location of inland objectives. This would position the units to advance inland in two or three columns, as was standard practice for offensive operations. Again, this differed from the Allied practice of first establishing a beachhead, from which to advance inland and to provide a base of operations. Another major difference between Japanese and Allied landings was that only short preparatory naval gunfire barrages were fired, often only after the landing troops were embarked, in contrast to prolonged Allied bombardments.

Often an SNLF, its size tailored for the specific operation, would serve as the first-wave assault troops to establish the initial landing site or seize a key objective. Army troops would follow it ashore or land simultaneously elsewhere to complete the operation. Landing craft would assemble in a column formation for their run ashore to provide more protection from fire. Stern lights aided orientation. Just short of shore the craft moved into a line formation. If opposition were expected they would open fire with machine guns during the approach. The assault troops would advance as quickly as possible across the beach to the nearest available cover. Assault companies and battalions did not maintain a reserve, all subunits were in the line. Machine-gun, infantry-gun, and mortar units would accompany the assault units since artillery could not be landed until later. The assault troops would move as quickly as possible to seize the initial objectives such as a port, airfield, town, garrison, or roads leading to objectives further inland. Infantry reserves, artillery, and engineers would follow ashore, transported by the first wave's returning landing craft. Once the senior Army commander ashore was certain he could hold the beaches, he assumed command of operations ashore, relieving the Navy occupation force commander of responsibility. During daylight more troops, service units, and at least 10-days' supplies would be landed. The transports would typically depart the area as soon as debarkation was completed for fear of air attack.

In the late-1920s the 5th, 11th, and 12th divisions were designated for amphibious training. These divisions were stationed near Ujina, Hiroshima's port, home of the IJA's Shipping Engineer Command and the port from which expeditionary forces were launched. These divisions were committed to China after the beginning of the China Incident. In 1937 the reactivated 18th Division replaced the 11th as an amphibious division. While these divisions conducted amphibious operations in China, most ended up in Manchuria. Only the 5th would see action in the Pacific War. Other divisions though were to conduct landings in China, such as the 3d, 6th, 16th, and 114th. Between 1937 and 1941 sixteen multiple-battalion to division-size landings were executed in China.

The IJA developed two types of landing craft in the late-1920s, the ramped *Daisatsu* (49ft, 100–120 troops) and the rampless *Kohatsu* (30ft, 40 troops). More advanced than any period landing craft, the IJA conducted no further development, and used these craft through the war. In contrast, Allied landing craft development continued throughout the war. Shipping engineer regiments operated these and other landing craft, each with 150–200 craft and up to 1,200 troops organized into three companies. Debarkation units consisted of some 1,000 troops, assisting the loading and unloading of transports.

Japanese landing operations relied heavily on manpower for offloading supplies and equipment. Motorization was limited. Here shipping engineers drag a truck ashore from a Type A landing barge.

Unit organization

While the Japanese basically adhered to a triangular organization concept, there were many exceptions found in all echelons. There were still square units with subunits organized in multiples of four. Most infantry battalions had four companies, but some had only three and others had five. German, French, and British unit organizational concepts may have influenced Japanese unit structure, but they very much adjusted unit organization to suit their needs. In regards to "standard" tables of organization, the Japanese could have two or more for any given unit as well as variations of these. It depended on what the unit's mission was and available resources when it was activated. The number of crew-served weapons assigned to a given unit might be less or more than the standard establishment.

Unit designation practices

The translation of Japanese unit designations was often corrupted early in the war as the interpreters, mostly Japanese-Americans (*Nisei*) with little military experience, would translate unit designations without reference to any common standard. This resulted in the same types of units sometimes being identified by two or three conflicting titles. Another problem was that some intelligence analysts attempted to assign Japanese units equivalent US designations giving them misleading functional titles.

IJA branches of service were divided into the Line Arms (*Heika*): infantry, artillery (field, mountain, medium, heavy, coast, AA), cavalry (horse, reconnaissance, tank), infantry mortar, engineer, chemical, transport (horse, motor), railway, meteorological, and air service. The Services (*Kakubu*) included the following: intendance, technical (ordnance), medical, veterinary, judicial, and military band.

Army level

"Groups of armies" were designated by names usually defining their area of operations (for example, the Southern, Kwantung, and China Expeditionary armies). The group of armies was roughly equivalent to an Allied theater of operation as it would cover forces responsible for a broad area. The North China Area Army existed prior to the war. It was not until the summer of 1942 that numbered area armies began to be activated. The "area army" (*Homengun*) roughly corresponded to an Allied field army, but was usually tied to its assigned area, in effect a sub-command of a group of armies. It consisted of one or more armies, air units, and would have some divisions and brigades under its direct control. The "army" (*Gun*) was equivalent to an Allied corps consisting of two to four divisions (some may have had only one or up to six) plus army troops (combat support and service units). Any number of independent mixed brigades might be assigned. Armies were numbered, but there were also named armies tied to their area of responsibility (such as the Chosen and Formosa armies, for example); these should not be confused with *Homengun* area armies. "District armies" were purely administrative commands controlling units in the Home Islands and responsible for mobilization, training, and forming new units.

Divisional level and below

Infantry divisions (*Saidan*) were numbered and did not include "infantry" within their designations. Divisions were not necessarily numbered in the

IJA parachute troops sleeve insignia. This insignia was seldom worn in combat.

Special Naval Landing Force parachute troops insignia.

The Imperial Guards Division displayed this insignia on their caps, as opposed to the simple star worn by other units.

sequence in which they were activated and some numbers were skipped. Depot divisions (*Rusu Saidan*) were found bearing the same numbers as infantry divisions. Divisions were sometimes known by their home district, such as the 2d or Sendai Division. Infantry regiments were originally assigned to divisions in numeric sequence, but over the years this changed as divisions were triangularized from 1936, with units deactivated, reactivated and reorganized. Divisions raised in the late-1930s and during the war were often assigned infantry regiments in numeric sequence. Infantry groups assigned to divisions and most divisional units bore the parent division's number. For the most part, divisional artillery regiments did not coincide with the division's number.

Regiments and independent battalions were numbered in sequence by branch or functional designation. The term "independent" (*Dokuritsu*) defined brigades, regiments, battalions, and smaller units not organic to divisions. "Mixed" (*Konset*) referred to a composite or combined arms unit rather than a unit comprising organic subunits of the same branch.

Infantry brigades organic to a square division, usually numbered in sequence, consisted of two infantry regiments. An independent mixed brigade (IMB) usually consisted of several independent infantry battalions (IIB) and organic artillery, engineer, and signal units.

Infantry and artillery regiments consisted of three organic battalions designated by Roman numbers (I–III). Allied intelligence usually identified them with Arabic numbers. Rifle and artillery companies were Arabic-numbered in sequence through the regiment or independent battalion. The Japanese did not use the term "battery" but rather "company." Allied intelligence usually designated artillery and AA companies as batteries though. Battalion machine-gun companies were designated, for example, Machine Gun Company, I Battalion, 16th Infantry. The same applied to companies organic to a regiment, for example, AT Company, 16th Infantry. Antiaircraft and some other types of regiments often had two battalions. In this book infantry, cavalry, reconnaissance, field artillery, mountain artillery, heavy artillery, tank, and engineer regimental designations do not include the word "regiment" (for example, 144th Infantry).

Tank, reconnaissance, cavalry, engineer, shipping engineer, signal, and many transport regiments were actually battalion-size, being composed of three to five companies and with no battalion structure. The nondescript term "unit" (*Tai* or *Butai*) is often encountered. A "unit" could range in size from a platoon to a battalion or larger support unit. They might be organic to a division, or an IMB, or be independent.

Table 3: unit designations	
Section	*Buntai* or *Han*
Platoon	*Shotai*
Company	*Chutai*
Battalion	*Daitai*
Unit	*Tai* or *Butai*
Regiment	*Rentai*
Group	*Dan*
Brigade	*Ryodan*
Division	*Shidan*
Army	*Gun*
Area Army	*Homengun*

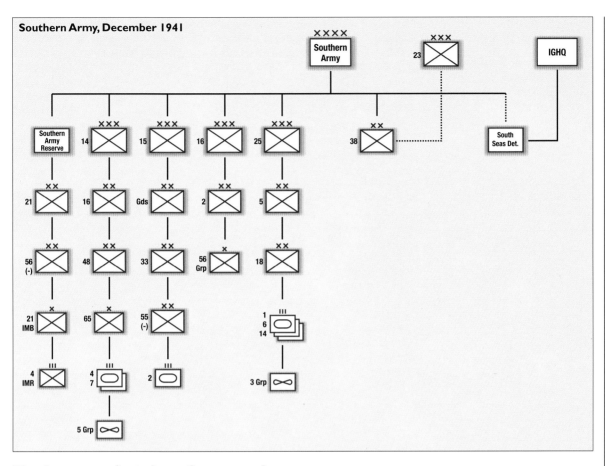

Southern Army, December 1941

Task organization for combat

The IJA maintained a flexible capability to tailor units for specific missions. There were no reservations with regard to attaching units from one formation to another in order to facilitate deployment and accomplish a given mission, even between divisions and regiments. With limited *matériel* resources, the Japanese pooled weapons in independent units that were assigned to area armies and armies. These units or detached subunits would be attached to divisions and smaller units as required by the mission. A deployed division could have well over a dozen smaller supporting units attached. There was no set standard, nor "habitual attachments."

Early in the war most triangular divisions still possessed an infantry group headquarters. This was often detached along with a single infantry regiment, artillery battalion, engineer company, and other supporting units to conduct an independent mission. It might be identified by its group designation or as a "detachment" preceded by the group commander's name; for example, Kimura Detachment. Reinforced regiments and battalions could also be detached for similar independent operations. Such special detachments (*Shitai*) were essentially task forces ranging in size from battalion to division. The Allies usually called them "forces" or "detachments." A number of such detachments were formed from detached regiments and battalions for use in the Southern Operations. During prolonged operations their attached units could change.

Platoons and sections from regimental AT, infantry-gun, and battalion machine-gun companies were attached to battalions and rifle companies as required. Support units from higher echelons were seldom allocated to subordinate units on an equal basis to the divisions within an army or to a division's regiments. The attachment of supporting units from army level and divisional level to a division's infantry regiments, for example, depended on each regiment's mission. The division did habitually attach an engineer company, medical unit (litter company, treatment and ambulance platoons), and radio and telephone sections to regiments.

The organization of divisions varied greatly and depended not only on the time and place activated, but the division's forecast mission. Japan's resources were such that it did not have the luxury of organizing all of its divisions as fully equipped, general purpose formations capable of performing all missions. Some "security divisions" (*Chian Shidan*) were organized with fewer heavy weapons and lacking certain support components, as they were intended for garrison (occupation), anti-bandit, or line-of-communication security. While on the one hand conserving resources, on the other it meant that less than capable divisions were deployed to combat zones when reinforcement was necessary. It also caused some difficulty in tactical planning and mission assignments as some of these divisions were not triangularly organized and were differently armed from the "standard" division. The 1st–20th (except 13th, 15th, 17th, 18th) divisions and the 2d Guards Division were considered permanent divisions (*Jo-setsu Shidan*). Others were classified as temporary divisions (*Tokusetsu Shidan*).

Three infantry divisions were motorized to some degree in January 1941. In addition to being trained for amphibious operations, the square 5th and 18th divisions and the triangular Guards Division received varying quantities of additional motor transport. The 5th had 860 trucks, making it the most heavily motorized, but it still had far fewer trucks than many European divisions. The 18th had even fewer and still relied heavily on horse-drawn artillery and transport. The Guards Division, smaller in strength, had 660 trucks. Due to this motorization, it was no accident that these divisions were committed to Malaya. The 48th had a slightly higher percentage of trucks as well. A standard triangular division at full complement had only 200 trucks; many possessed far less.

Triangular divisions (*San-tan-i Shidan*) were first proposed in 1921 and called for the elimination of the two brigade headquarters, deactivation of one regiment and the reduction of the battalions' four companies to three—a net saving of approximately six divisions of troops. Considered too drastic a reduction, only one company was cut from each infantry battalion and one company from each cavalry regiment, reducing the Army by 60,0000 men. The cost savings allowed a machine-gun company to be added to each infantry regiment and cavalry brigade raised.

The deactivation of five divisions in 1925 resulted in serious morale problems for officers, who were assigned to a regiment for life. Only small numbers of officers achieved general officer rank and higher staff assignments. Unit officers were seconded to training and school assignments, but usually returned to their parent regiment. Officers of the deactivated regiments were reassigned to others, but always felt like outsiders. This problem was encountered again during the war when units were split from the parent regiments and divisions as expeditionary units, or used to form new units.

The 1940 standard B infantry division

On paper, the 1940 standard B, or *Otsu*, triangular infantry division consisted of 20,000 troops, although this could be anything from 18,000–21,000 troops. This depended on the specific assigned units, as there were several alternatives.

The division HQ consisted of the general staff and administrative staff sections plus small guard, signal, ordnance, and veterinary detachments along with a small HQ train for transport and baggage. The infantry group (*Hoheidan*) HQ, in direct charge of the three infantry regiments, had an administrative staff, guard detachment, and small HQ train. Some infantry groups had a tankette company (*Keisokosha Chutai*) with 10–17 machine gun-armed tankettes.

Table 4: standard B infantry division

Standard unit	Strength (officer/EM/total)	Alternate unit	Strength (officer/EM/total)
Division HQ	50/250/300		
Infantry group HQ[1]	10/85/95	*May have been deleted*	
Tankette company	c.80–120 total	*May have been deleted*	
Infantry regiment (x3)[2]	113/3,732/3,845	Infantry regiment (x3)[3]	101/3,174/3,275
		Artillery group HQ[4]	c.160 total
FA regiment	80/2,020/2,100	Mountain artillery regt	91/3,409/3,500
Recon regiment	20/580/600	Cavalry regiment	46/904/950
		Tankette company[5]	c.80–120 total
Engineer regiment	25/925/950		
Transport regiment	50/1,760/1,810		
Signal unit	8/232/240		
Ordnance duty unit	6/104/110		
Division medical service			
Medical unit	40/1,070/1,110		
Field hospital (x4)	25/225/250		
Water supply unit	11/224/235		
Veterinary hospital	10/105/115		
Total	**724/19,276/20,000**		

Notes
[1] *Guards, 2d, 21st, 38th, 48th, and 56th divisions only.*
[2] *Battalions with four rifle companies.*
[3] *Battalions with three rifle companies.*
[4] *Assigned only to Guards and 2d divisions.*
[5] *Normally assigned to the infantry group.*

Standard B triangular infantry division

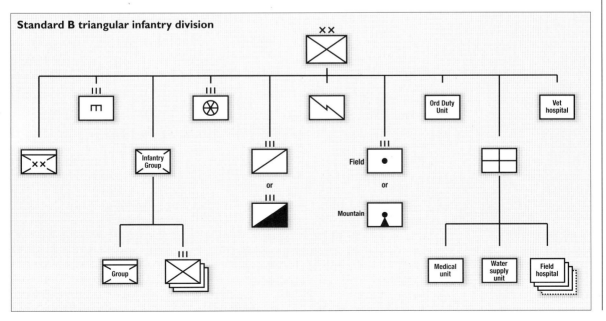

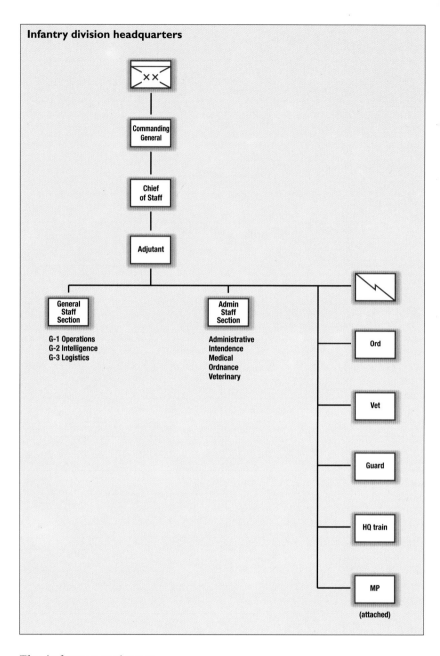

Infantry division headquarters

Commanding General

Chief of Staff

Adjutant

General Staff Section

G-1 Operations
G-2 Intelligence
G-3 Logistics

Admin Staff Section

Administrative
Intendence
Medical
Ordnance
Veterinary

Ord

Vet

Guard

HQ train

MP

(attached)

The infantry regiment

The infantry regiment (*Hohei Rentai*), comprising roughly 3,800 troops and over 700 horses, was a well-balanced unit requiring few attachments to be effective in combat. Its basic organization remained constant throughout the war, but many variations of subunit internal organization and the types and allocation of crew-served weapons can be found. Organic medical support was light, with two surgeons and two orderlies in the regimental administrative section, three surgeons and four orderlies in each battalion, and four orderlies in each company. Additional medical support was attached from the division.

It must be noted that the following strength figures represent typical unit strength; the actual strength in the field varied greatly and few intelligence documents agree with each other on this matter. Note also that when numbers are provided the first number refers to officers and the second to NCOs and enlisted men. Where only one number is shown, it refers to NCOs and enlisted men.

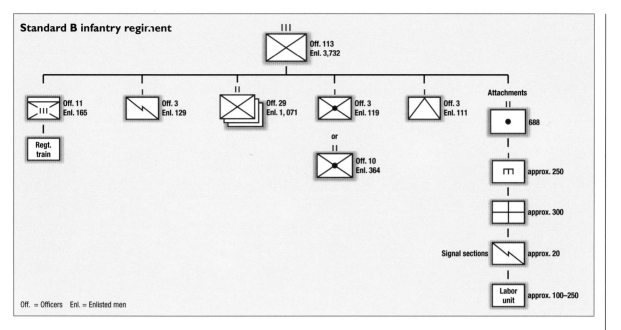

Standard B infantry regiment

Off. = Officers   Enl. = Enlisted men

REGIMENTAL HQ

The regimental HQ consisted of the staff, administrative (2/16), code and intelligence (1/10), ordnance (1/8), intendance (1/4), and LMG sections (5) plus a color guard (1/5). The staff, such that it was, consisted only of the commander, operations officer, adjutant, and gas officer. It also included a 121-man regimental train with field and ammunition sections. The 40-man field section had 30 one-horse two-wheel carts or 40 packhorses. It carried a day's rations for the regimental companies along with headquarters supplies and equipment. A field kitchen from the division might be attached. The 81-man ammunition section carried a day's supply of ammunition for the entire regiment in some 60 two-wheel horse carts or on 120 packhorses.

THE INFANTRY BATTALION

The three, roughly 1,100-man infantry battalions (*Hohei Daitai*) had a 30-man HQ with a commander and adjutant, administrative (4/14), code and intelligence (3), ordnance and intendance (2/3), liaison (4), and LMG sections (5). The 110-man battalion train had a 50-man field section and a 60-man ammunition section with horse carts or packhorses. The battalion trains were sometimes combined with the regimental train. A labor unit of 100–200 men organized into six sections plus an equipment section augmented some regiments. This was by no means a standard fixture. More often than not, labor details were drawn from the infantry battalions or from external labor units.

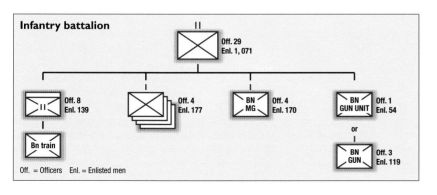

Infantry battalion

Off. = Officers   Enl. = Enlisted men

29

THE RIFLE COMPANY

The four, 180-man rifle companies had a 19-man HQ with the commander, a personnel warrant officer (equivalent to an executive or administrative officer), a sergeant major in charge of personnel records (roughly equating to a first-

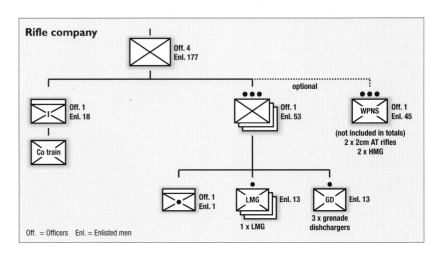

Rifle company

Off. 4
Enl. 177

Off. 1
Enl. 18

Co train

optional

Off. 1
Enl. 53

WPNS   Off. 1
       Enl. 45

(not included in totals)
2 x 2cm AT rifles
2 x HMG

Off. 1
Enl. 1

LMG   Enl. 13

1 x LMG

GD   Enl. 13

3 x grenade
dishchargers

Off. = Officers   Enl. = Enlisted men

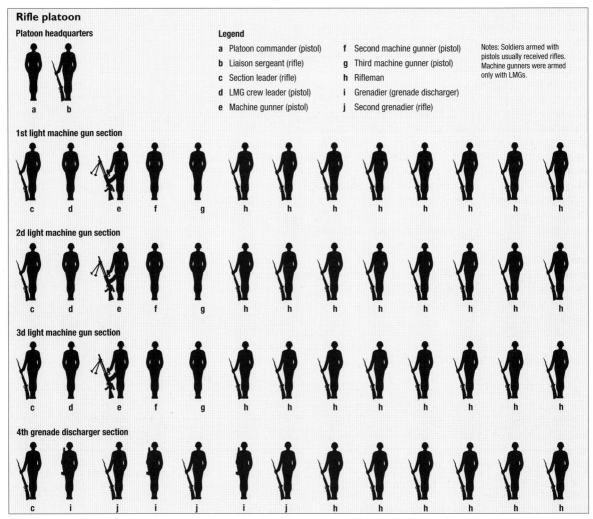

Rifle platoon

Platoon headquarters

a   b

Legend

a   Platoon commander (pistol)
b   Liaison sergeant (rifle)
c   Section leader (rifle)
d   LMG crew leader (pistol)
e   Machine gunner (pistol)

f   Second machine gunner (pistol)
g   Third machine gunner (pistol)
h   Rifleman
i   Grenadier (grenade discharger)
j   Second grenadier (rifle)

Notes: Soldiers armed with pistols usually received rifles. Machine gunners were armed only with LMGs.

1st light machine gun section

c   d   e   f   g   h   h   h   h   h   h   h   h

2d light machine gun section

c   d   e   f   g   h   h   h   h   h   h   h   h

3d light machine gun section

c   d   e   f   g   h   h   h   h   h   h   h   h

4th grenade discharger section

c   i   j   i   j   i   j   h   h   h   h   h

sergeant), a supply sergeant, an arms and equipment sergeant, four medical orderlies, an officer's orderly, bugler, and eight messengers. The three, 54-man rifle platoons had a two-man HQ with a platoon commander and a liaison sergeant. Roughly equating to a US platoon sergeant, the latter's main duty was to ensure orders were relayed to the sections through arm signals and messengers. The three, 13-man light machine-gun sections were led by corporals. Each consisted of eight riflemen and a four-man machine-gun crew: the latter consisted of a crew leader, machine gunner, and second and third gunners (ammunition bearers). All four of the crew were armed with pistols, but in practice often carried rifles. One rifleman usually carried a rifle-grenade launcher. Sections assigned to strengthened units had the addition of a two-man 5cm grenade-discharger crew. Designating the section "light machine-gun" rather than "rifle" emphasized the focus on the machine gun as the fire base for the section, and the role of the riflemen in protecting it. The grenade-discharger section was led by a corporal and had three, two-man grenade-discharger crews plus six riflemen, who also carried ammunition. The grenadiers were armed only with the discharger and a bayonet, but some may have carried rifles. Ten- to twelve-man sections were common. In combat, when strength dwindled the grenade-discharger section was usually absorbed into the LMG sections.

Some battalions had only three rifle companies, though most still had four early in the war. Though not a normal fixture, some strengthened companies had a 46-man weapons platoon. This would have two HMGs and two 2cm AT rifles, each manned by an 11-man section. If such a platoon were assigned, the weapons were re-allocated from the battalion machine-gun company and infantry-gun platoon, as opposed to having the allocation increased.

OTHER BATTALION- AND REGIMENTAL-LEVEL UNITS

The standard 174-man battalion machine-gun company had a 14-man HQ and three machine-gun platoons. The platoons had a two-man HQ and four 11-man sections, each with an HMG for a total of 12, but some had only eight HMGs. There was also a 22-man ammunition platoon. Complete platoons might be attached to the forward companies or pairs of guns might be attached. Some HMGs were retained under battalion control. Battalions featuring company weapons platoons, with two HMGs assigned to each, were organized into two, 24-man HMG platoons of two sections each plus a 15-man ammunition platoon.

The 55-man battalion gun platoon had a 10-man HQ, a 15-man ammunition section, and two 15-man gun sections, each with a 7cm infantry gun. A few units possessed a 122-man battalion gun company, a 27-man ammunition platoon, and two 31-man gun platoons, each with two 7cm infantry guns. Units fortunate enough to be provided 2cm AT rifles would also have four AT rifle platoons added to the gun company along with an enlarged 39-man ammunition platoon. Each 24-man platoon had a two-man HQ and two 11-man sections, each manning an AT rifle. These platoons did not exist if the AT rifles were assigned to rifle company weapons platoons.

Several company-size units were directly under regimental control, enhancing its combat capabilities. The 122-man regimental gun company had a 25-man HQ, an observation section, a 31-man ammunition platoon, and three 33-man gun platoons. Gun platoons had two 15-man gun sections, each with a 7.5cm infantry gun. A few regiments had 364-man regimental gun battalions with two, 170-man, four-gun companies and a 24-man HQ.

The regimental AT company had 122 men in a 20-man HQ, a 21-man ammunition platoon, and three 25-man AT gun platoons, each with two 3.7cm AT guns manned by 11-man sections. Some low-priority units had two 3.7cm AT guns in the regimental gun company along with only two 7.5cm regimental guns.

The 132-man regimental signal company was organized into a 30-man HQ, a telephone platoon with four to six sections each with three telephones and a switchboard, and a radio platoon with five to eight sections, each operating one radio. The telephone and radio sections were attached to battalions and regimental companies.

Table 5: standard B infantry regiment		
	Strength	**Main weapons**
Regimental HQ with train	11/165[1]	4 x LMGs
Regimental infantry gun company	3/119	6 x 7.5cm infantry guns
Regimental antitank company	3/111	6 x 3.7cm AT guns
Regimental signal company	3/129	
Infantry battalion (x3)	29/1,071	
Battalion HQ with train	8/139	1 x LMG
Rifle company (x4)	4/177	9 x LMGs, 9 grenade dischargers
Battalion machine-gun company	4/170	12 x HMGs
Gun platoon or company	1/54 or 3/119	2 or 4 x 7cm infantry guns
Attachments		
Artillery battalion (occasionally)		
Engineer company from divisional engineer regiment		
Regimental medical unit from divisional medical service		
Signal sections from divisional signal unit		
Labor unit (optional)		
Notes: [1] *The first number refers to officers and the second to NCOs and enlisted men.*		

Field and mountain artillery regiments

The 2,322-man field artillery (FA) regiment (*Yahohei Rentai*) had a very small HQ, an observation group, a regimental train with a field and three ammunition sections, and three 688-man artillery battalions. These had a small HQ, observation group, battalion train, and three artillery companies. A company had an HQ, observation group, company train, and two platoons, each with two 7.5cm guns manned by 19 men, giving a total of 36 howitzers. There were about 2,000 horses assigned to the regiment for towing guns, and ammunition and baggage carts. The regimental, battalion, and company observation groups had observation and signal platoons, which became progressively smaller at each echelon. Some regiments may have had one 7.5cm battalion replaced by a 10cm howitzer battalion. The 3,400-man mountain artillery regiment (*Sampohei*

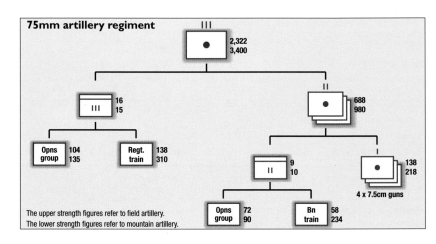

A mountain artillery unit transporting a 7.5cm Type 94 (1934) gun could cover up to 10–15 miles a day. While much slower than motorized transport, packhorse units could travel across terrain impassable to trucks, such as swamps, jungles, and mountains. A packhorse could carry a little under 300 lbs. The drawback was that packhorse units required more manpower and large quantities of fodder, resulting in supply problems.

Rentai) was organized much the same way as the FA regiment. It was equipped with thirty-six 7.5cm mountain guns, which were transported by 1,400 draft and packhorses. A crew of 24 manned each mountain gun.

Reconnaissance and cavalry regiments

The 730-man reconnaissance regiment (*Sobaku Rentai*) was a cavalry-branch unit, which gradually replaced the cavalry regiment as the war progressed. It consisted of a 130-man HQ and train, a mounted company, two truck-borne companies, a tankette or armored car company, and a truck transport company. The 130-man mounted company had four 30-man platoons. Few regiments actually possessed the tankette or armored car company. A regimental company had either seven tankettes or armored cars. The 160-man truck-borne companies had two 50-man platoons organized and armed essentially the same as a rifle platoon, a 24-man machine-gun platoon with two HMGs, and a 24-man AT platoon with two 3.7cm AT guns—which many units lacked. The 100-man truck transport company had two platoons, at least on paper, with one to transport each truck-borne company.

The 950-man divisional cavalry regiment (*Kihei Rentai*) had an 82-man HQ and train, a machine-gun, and three rifle and saber companies. The companies had three platoons each armed with three LMGs and two grenade dischargers plus a machine-gun platoon with two HMGs. The machine-gun company had two platoons each with two HMGs and two 2cm AT rifles plus a platoon of two 3.7cm AT guns and an ammunition platoon. Although supplied with some 1,100 horses, it was not uncommon for these units to be dismounted later in the war.

Engineer, transport, and signals units

The 900–1,000-man engineer regiment (*Kohei Rentai*) had a 100-man HQ and train and a *matériel* platoon of 50–100 troops. The three engineer companies had approximately 250 men in four 50-man platoons plus a 25-man *matériel* section with trucks and some powered engineer equipment. The platoons had four sections each. A company was habitually attached to each infantry regiment to provide basic obstacle clearing, light road repairs, footbridge construction, and other minor tasks. Non-divisional engineer regiments were attached to divisions from army level for more specialized engineering tasks.

Transport regiment (*Shichohei Rentai*) organization varied greatly depending on the number of trucks available. Ideally it consisted of a truck transport battalion and a draft transport battalion. The truck battalion had two or three companies, each with up to 50 trucks of 1.5-ton capacity. Many had fewer and some virtually none other than commandeered vehicles. The draft battalion had three or four companies, each with some 240, two-wheel, single-horse-drawn carts and 350

The IJA fielded a wide variety of specialized engineer units. Hand tools were used for much of the work, but some powered equipment was available, like this German-built, 1928-model, diesel-powered, 8-ton road roller. The scarcity of equipment forced the Japanese to limit the extent of their construction projects.

ABOVE Truck transport was in short supply, and in Japanese divisions was on a much lower scale than in their European counterparts. A commonly used 1.5-ton cargo track was the Isuzu Type 94 (1934). The rear wheels were powered, but not the front ones, which limited its cross-country mobility.

RIGHT 61st Infantry troops cover an engineer as he sprays a Corregidor bunker with a Type 93 (1934) flamethrower. Since the Japanese did not use thickened fuel, its range was only 25–30 yds.

The primary means of tactical transport found at all levels was the one-horse, two-wheel cart, which could carry 400–500 lbs of cargo. Here additional mules have been hitched to the cart to drag it through mud. In occupied areas, every motorized vehicle was confiscated for military use.

troops. Many regiments did not possess a battalion structure, but had up to eight draft companies plus a small veterinary unit. Such an eight-company regiment normally allocated four companies for rations and forage, two for artillery ammunition, and one for small-arms ammunition. In some units packhorse companies substituted draft companies on the basis of two packhorse companies for one draft. They had 300 packhorses and 450 troops. About one-third of the troops were armed.

The large company-size signal unit (*Denshintai*) had two telephone, one radio, and a *matériel* platoon plus a 20-man HQ and messenger section. The 50-man telephone platoons each had four sections operating two telephones and a switchboard. The 100-man radio platoon had between eight and twelve sections, each operating a radio. The wire and radio sections were detailed to regiments and other divisional units. Artillery units possessed organic signal elements though. The company-size ordnance duty unit provided weapon repair and technical services.

Medical and veterinary services

The division medical service, headed by a colonel, was sizeable in order to treat casualties in forward areas. This allowed the wounded an earlier return to duty and reduced evacuation requirements. It included a medical staff section in the division staff. The divisional medical unit (*Shidan Eiseitai*), commanded by a colonel or lieutenant-colonel, had a 265-man headquarters providing various specialized medical, dental, and pharmaceutical services plus three treatment platoons, three litter companies (20 litter teams), and an ambulance company (45 ambulances). A litter company, treatment platoon, and ambulance platoon formed a regimental medical unit for attachment to each infantry regiment.

Table 6: Southern Operations triangular divisions

Division	Infantry regts	Artillery regt	Recon/cavalry regt	Engineer regt	Transport regt
Guards	3, 4, 5 Guards	Guards FA	Guards Recon	Guards	Guards
2d	4, 16, 29	2 FA	2 Recon	2	2
4th	8, 37, 61	4 FA	4 Cavalry	4	4
16th	9, 20, 33	22 FA	16 Recon	16	16
21st	62, 82, 83	51 Mountain	Tankette Co [1]	21	21
33d	216, 217, 218	33 Mountain	—	33	33
38th	228, 229, 230	38 Mountain	Tankette Co [1]	38	38
48th	1, 2 Formosa, 47	47 Mountain	47 Cavalry	47	47
55th	112, 143, 144	55 Mountain	55 Cavalry	55	55
56th	113, 146, 148	56 FA	56 Recon, Tankette Co[1]	56	56

Notes:
[1] Designated, for example, Tankette Company, 56th Infantry Group.

They provided collection, initial treatment, and evacuation to the field hospitals for wounded soldiers. The three or four, 500-patient field hospitals (*Yasen Byoin*, designated 1st–4th in each division) each had a medical company to operate the hospital, perform surgery, and treat the sick and wounded. It also had a transport company to haul equipment, supplies, and personnel. It provided manpower to establish the hospital facilities in tents. The large water-supply and purification unit located, purified, and distributed water supplies as well as performing many preventive medical and field hygiene tasks.

The company-size veterinary hospital treated sick, injured, and wounded horses. It was also responsible for advising on the care and feeding of the division's 7,500 horses, as even a few hundred ill horses could reduce a division's effectiveness. Few medical and veterinary troops were armed.

The square infantry division

The few remaining square divisions (*Yon-tan-I Shidan*) were quite large, comprising some 25,000 troops. They were holdovers after the 1936 reorganization when the process of triangularization got underway for most divisions. They had two infantry brigade (*Hohei Ryodan*) HQs, each with two infantry regiments (not to be confused with the "brigaded division" of two brigades with four IIBs apiece, which will be discussed in a subsequent volume). The 5th Division's 5th FA Regiment had two 7.5cm battalions and a 10cm howitzer battalion, which were truck-drawn. The 18th Division's 18th Mountain Artillery had three battalions of pack-transported 7.5cm mountain guns. Component units were similar to the triangular divisions, but slightly higher in strength and possessed more truck transport. The motorized 22d Cavalry Battalion (*22 Kihei Daitai*) was smaller than a cavalry regiment with 600 troops. The 5th Division was triangularized in early-1942 with the detachment of the 41st Infantry. The 18th was reorganized in April 1943 with the 124th Infantry detached and the 22d Cavalry Battalion disbanded. Both divisions dropped the brigade HQs.

Division	Infantry brigades	Infantry regts	Artillery regt	Recon/cavalry unit	Engineer regt	Transport regt
5th	9	11, 41	5 FA	5 Recon Regt.	5	5
	21	21, 42				
18th	23	55, 56	18 Mountain	22 Cavalry Bn.	12	12
	35	114, 124				

Table 7: Southern Operations square divisions

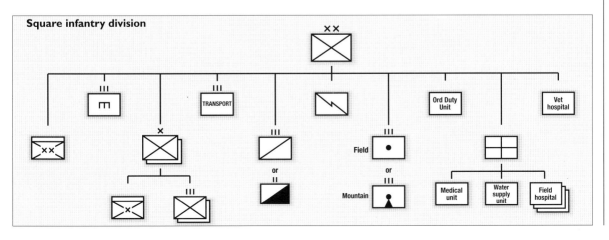

Square infantry division

Independent brigades

The concept of the independent mixed brigade (IMB, *Dokuritsu Konset Ryodan*) stretched back to 1894, when the deployment of troops to Korea was considered to force a confrontation with China. A sufficiently strong force was deemed necessary in order to inflict enough damage on the Chinese, with the aim of provoking them into sending more troops. Fearing the Prime Minister would reject the deployment of a strong force, an Army general suggested to the Foreign Minister that only a "brigade" be sent, typically comprising 2,000 men—but this would be a "mixed brigade" reinforced with additional infantry, cavalry, artillery, and service troops, totaling 7–8,000 men.

IMBs were mainly intended for occupation duty and line-of-communication security. Most had from three to six 1,000-man independent infantry battalions (IIB, *Dokuritsu Hohei Daitai*), with five being typical, giving the IMB 6,150 men. It also had a 160-man HQ, 600-man battalion-size FA unit, 250-man engineer unit, and 140-man signal unit. Other infantry brigade-sized units included independent infantry brigades (*Dokuritsu Hohei Ryodan*) with four IIBs and no support units; independent infantry groups (*Dokuritsu Hoheidan*) with three divisional-type infantry regiments and no support units (which later provided core troops for new divisions); independent mixed regiments (*Dokuritsu Konset Rentai*); and independent infantry regiments (*Dokuritsu Hohei Rentai*).

The two brigades employed in the Southern Operations featured a different organization though. The 5,000-man 21st IMB, instead of IIBs, was assigned the 3,360-man 170th Infantry Regiment; a 140-man HQ, 360-man artillery unit; engineer and signal units as other IMBs; a 130-man tank unit with 11 light tanks; a 110-man 2cm AA unit; a 260-man transport unit; and a 250-man field hospital.

The 6,659-man 65th Brigade (*65 Ryodan*, no other descriptive designation in its title) was a unique unit consisting of the 1,920-man 122d, 141st, and 142d infantry regiments. They initially had only two battalions and a gun company apiece and lacked an AT company. The 65th was assigned company-size engineer and medical units, and a platoon-size signal unit.

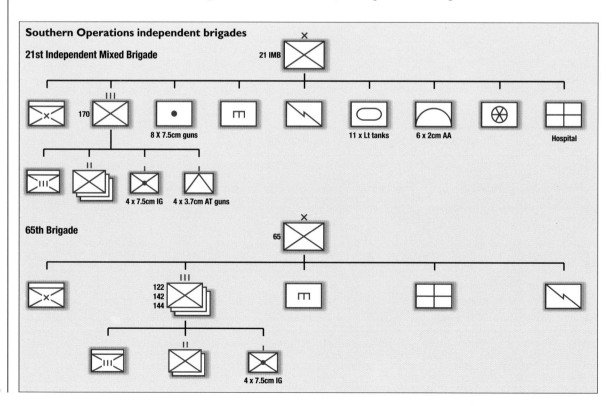

Tank regiments

Battalion-size tank regiments (*Sensha Rentai*) varied in internal organization. They could consist of 700–850 troops and 30-plus to 50-plus tanks. The three or four tank companies might have been light, medium, or mixed. A standard regiment had one medium and two light tanks in the HQ; the 1st or 4th Company had one light tank in the HQ and four platoons of three light tanks each; and the other companies had three platoons with three medium tanks plus one medium and two light tanks in the HQ. This gave it 21 light and 31 medium tanks. Some regiments eliminated the light company assigning a light platoon to each medium company. Light tanks were used for scouting and

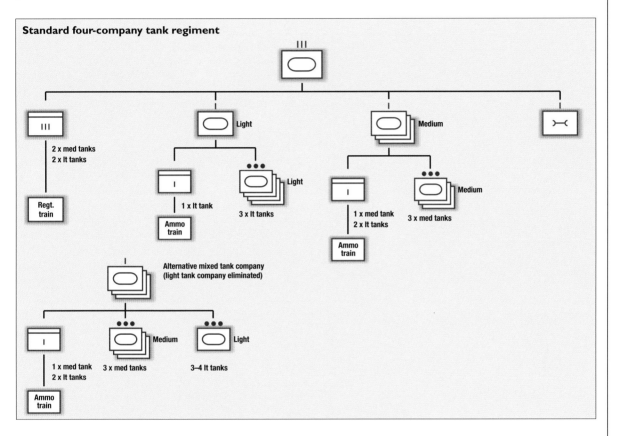

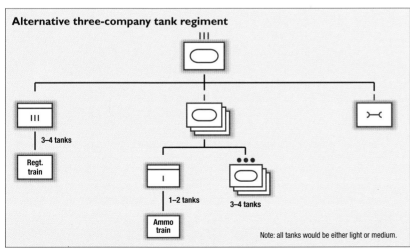

flank security. Some company HQs may have had one or two tankettes in lieu of light tanks. There were instances of platoons having four or five tanks, while other regiments were understrength. A few regiments had only three light companies with three platoons apiece. The regiment possessed a truck-borne maintenance company and each tank company had a motorized ammunition (and baggage) train.

The regiments in Malaya were under the 3d Tank Group (*3 Senshadan*, incorrectly called a "brigade"). Groups were administrative headquarters inadequate for tactical control and were eliminated in 1942. The tank regiments employed in the Southern Operations varied greatly in terms of their compliment and internal organization, as shown in Table 8.

Table 8: Southern Operations tank regiments		
Malaya		
1st Tank	37 x Type 97 medium tanks	Col Mukaida
	20 x Type 95 light tanks	
6th Tank	37 x Type 97 medium tanks	Col Kawamura
	20 x Type 95 light tanks	
14th Tank	45 x Type 95 light tanks	Col Kita
Philippines[1]		
4th Tank	38 x Type 95 light tanks	LtCol Kumagaya
7th Tank	34 x Type 94 medium tanks	Col Sonoda
	2 x Type 97 medium tanks	
	14 x Type 95 light tanks	
Netherlands East Indies[2]		
2d Tank (-)	31 x Type 97 medium tanks	Col Mori
	5 x M3 light tanks (captured)	
Burma[3]		
1st Company, 2d Tank	12 x Type 95 light tanks	Lt Okada

Notes:
[1] Some captured US M3 light tanks were also employed.
[2] 4th Tank Regiment arrived later from the Philippines.
[3] 1st and 4th Tank regiments arrived in April 1942.

A 7th Tank Regiment Type 94 (1934) medium tank crosses a hastily repaired bridge en route to Manila. The white five-pointed star identified the 1st Company. The 3d Company used a star with round "points" and the 4th Company (Light) used the below insignia:

Tactics

The close-combat traditions of the *samurai* essentially lived on as Japan entered the modern age. The arrival of repeating rifles, machine guns, and breech-loading artillery did little to diminish this. When new field manuals were published in 1909, the infantry manual emphasized the infantry attack preceded by a barrage of rifle fire followed by a bayonet charge. Regardless of the lessons learned at Port Arthur, where Japanese troops were mown down by machine guns and artillery in World War I fashion, combined arms warfare was secondary. The other branch manuals focused solely on supporting the infantry attack.

Machine guns were located only at regimental level until 1924 when the light machine gun was fielded, much later than issued at squad level in Western armies. The principles of close combat with the bayonet, advancing in skirmish lines, and direct-fire artillery were adhered to long after they were abandoned in the West. However, it must be said that Japanese quickly embraced the light machine gun as a principal infantry weapon and developed all their small-unit tactics around it. This was especially apparent in the Pacific when, coupled with the grenade discharger and protected by riflemen, these weapons created havoc among Allied troops in close-range jungle firefights.

Even in open terrain the Japanese emphasized closing rapidly with the enemy and engaging him in close combat, to exploit their superior *seishin*. When facing Allied forces this "hugging" tactic had the added benefit of lessening any artillery and close air support advantage for fear of causing friendly casualties. The rugged terrain and dense vegetation encountered in much of the Pacific and Southeast Asia provided an ideal, if harsh and unforgiving, environment for close-combat tactics. While most armies might sanction night attacks, the IJA was one of the few that practiced them aggressively and accomplished them successfully on a regular basis.

Envelopment and encirclement

The IJA placed great trust in the enveloping attack, which might take one of several forms: single envelopment to one flank, double envelopment to both flanks, and encirclement. Envelopments attacked the enemy's flank(s), while encirclement drove deeper to cut the enemy off from the rear (sometimes from only one flank). At the same time pressure was applied to the enemy's front and flanks.

A paratrooper of the 1st Raiding Force mans a 7.7mm Type 99 (1939) LMG. This two-regiment IJA unit executed jumps at Palembang, Sumatra and Koepang, Timor in February 1942.

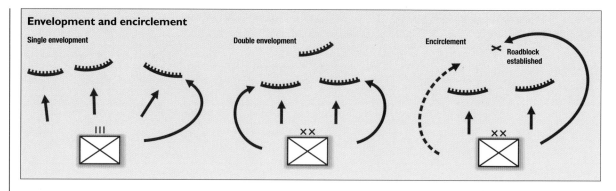

Envelopment and encirclement

Single envelopment

Double envelopment

Encirclement

Roadblock established

Encirclement required a division-sized or larger force. Divisions and regiments could conduct single and double envelopments. The size of the Japanese force and its exact deployment obviously depended on the strength, deployment, and composition of the enemy as well as the terrain. The Japanese would often execute envelopments with forces numerically smaller than the Allies would have used though.

The most common method of conducting an envelopment was to advance in two or three parallel columns. When contact was made with the enemy, one or two columns would move to attack the flanks or rear. This was the common means of an advance to engagement by a division. A brigade or regiment might advance in one or two columns until making contact. The lead elements would place pressure on the enemy's front, a holding attack, while following units would encircle to one or both flanks. Another, though more complex method, was to engage the enemy and move units through concealing terrain or under the cover of darkness to attack the flanks. Even a rifle platoon, when meeting an enemy force, was to conduct a holding attack while one section attacked from the flank.

In Southeast Asia, the NEI, and Philippines the Japanese would conduct enveloping movements 2–3 miles to the flanks of the Allied force and several miles deep. They would establish battalion- and larger-sized roadblocks on the line-of-communications, and Allied units, finding such a large force in their rear and lacking sufficient reserves, were forced to withdraw frontline units to deal with the new threat. The Japanese to the front would then conduct direct or infiltration attacks on the weakened force. Infiltrating platoons, when counterattacked, would simply go to ground in the dense vegetation, allow the attack to pass through, and engage the enemy from behind.

Frontal attack

The IJA cautioned against the frontal attack, but in practice the Japanese frequently executed it. This was often due to the overzealous desire to annihilate the enemy, but terrain and enemy dispositions might also prevent an enveloping attack. Infiltration and probes to locate weak sectors would precede the main assault, and the main attack would strike here. The goal was to penetrate deep into the enemy's rear and attack command posts, artillery, and services. Tanks would be employed if available. Artillery support was usually inadequate and maximum use would be made of heavy machine guns, infantry guns, and mortars.

The division would normally advance in two columns, with a reinforced regiment in each. The reserve regiment would move behind one of the lead columns, depending on which flank the commander had anticipated would be the most effective to envelop from. If moving in three columns the third column, situated on either flank as a screen or security force, usually consisted of a reinforced battalion, which may have been detached from one of the lead regiments or the reserve. These columns might have been designated the left,

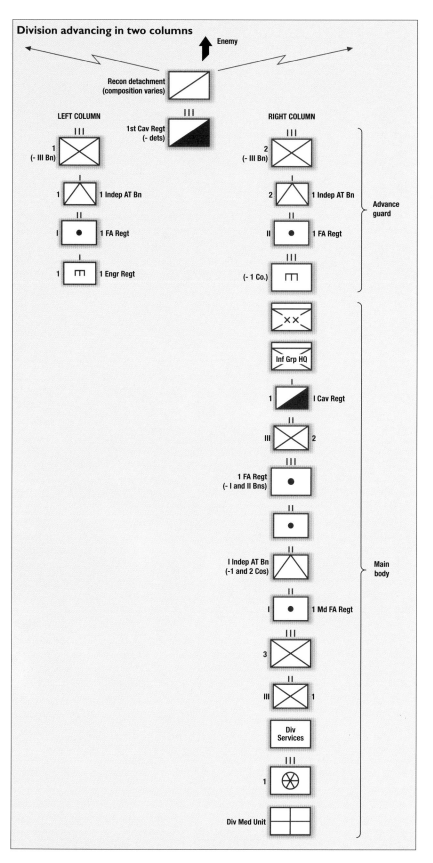

Division advancing in two columns

Enemy

Recon detachment
(composition varies)

LEFT COLUMN

1st Cav Regt
(- dets)

RIGHT COLUMN

1
(- III Bn)

2
(- III Bn)

1   1 Indep AT Bn

2   1 Indep AT Bn

Advance
guard

I   1 FA Regt

II   1 FA Regt

1   1 Engr Regt

(- 1 Co.)

Inf Grp HQ

1   I Cav Regt

III   2

1 FA Regt
(- I and II Bns)

I Indep AT Bn
(-1 and 2 Cos)

Main
body

I   1 Md FA Regt

3

III   1

Div
Services

1

Div Med Unit

This diagram shows a division
advancing in two columns. In this
situation, the division commander
has assessed that it will be beneficial
to envelop the enemy's left flank
using his right column. The unit
designations shown are notional,
and do not represent a particular
division.

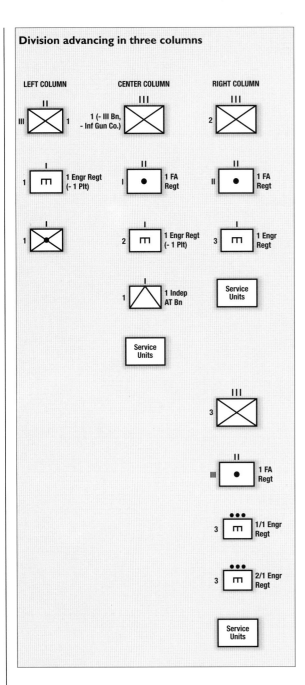

Division advancing in three columns

LEFT COLUMN

III 1 | ⊠ || 1 (– III Bn, – Inf Gun Co.)

1 | ⊓ (I) | 1 Engr Regt (– 1 Plt)

1 | ⊠ (●) (I)

Service Units

CENTER COLUMN

III ⊠

I | ● (II) | 1 FA Regt

2 | ⊓ (I) | 1 Engr Regt (– 1 Plt)

1 | ⊠/ (I) | 1 Indep AT Bn

Service Units

III ⊠ 3

III | ● (II) | 1 FA Regt

3 | ⊓ (●●●) | 1/1 Engr Regt

3 | ⊓ (●●●) | 2/1 Engr Regt

Service Units

RIGHT COLUMN

2 | ⊠ (III)

II | ● (II) | 1 FA Regt

3 | ⊓ (I) | 1 Engr Regt

Service Units

This diagram shows a division advancing in three columns. The unit designations shown are notional, and do not represent a particular division.

center, and right wings or units. An advance guard of up to battalion strength preceded each column, from which it was detached. The column most likely to engage the main enemy force might be more heavily reinforced than the other(s). The reconnaissance or cavalry regiment would provide a reconnaissance detachment, advancing even further ahead. It would also provide flank-screening detachments. The division commander would maintain direct control over the column most likely to engage the enemy, its advance guard, the reconnaissance detachment, and the division main body following that column. This included the infantry group headquarters, reserve regiment, and service units. The other column and its advance guard were under the control of the regimental commander. Each column was reinforced by artillery, engineer, and medical units and, depending on the threat, AA and AT subunits.

Once the enemy had been located and contact was imminent, the columns would deploy their subunits forward in phases, in a coordinated deployment:

Bunshin	Break from march column into smaller columns while out of artillery range and continue to advance.
Tenkai	Deploy on a line of departure for a coordinated attack.
Sokai	Advance from the line of departure in sections and platoons.
Sankai	Final deployment with units arranged to attack by close assault.

Regardless of the benefits of such coordinated attacks, the Japanese tended to execute piecemeal attacks in both exercises and combat. Most armies discourage piecemeal attacks because of the low chance of success owing to local attacks being conducted at different times, a lack of critical mass, and little coordination between attacking units. They should only be conducted if (1) the objective is limited; (2) insufficient time is available; and/or (3) the attacker is vastly superior to the defender. The Japanese, in contrast, prescribed the piecemeal attack in doctrine. They adhered to the first two points above, but frequently attacked superior, well-prepared enemy forces. While this was frequently successful in China and against ill-prepared Allied forces in 1941–42, it later led to disaster.

Tank and artillery coordination

The Japanese viewed tanks mainly as infantry support weapons. Like artillery they were most effective if deployed in the front alongside the infantry. There was no instruction for them to be massed or to engage in battles with enemy armor. Major efforts would be made to position tanks with the attacking infantry in secrecy. Tank companies and platoons were usually attached directly to infantry battalions and seldom employed in larger formations.

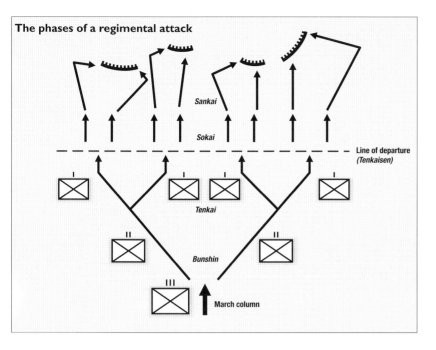

The phases of a regimental attack

Sankai

Sokai

Line of departure
(*Tenkaisen*)

Tenkai

Bunshin

March column

The tanks' missions were to breach wire obstacles and destroy crew-served weapon positions. Tanks were not necessarily viewed as decisive weapons, but strictly as aids to the infantry. As a result, the infantry was told to continue its advance if the tanks were knocked out.

One of Japan's greatest areas of deficiency was in its artillery. This applied not only to the limited capabilities of Japanese artillery, but also to its quantity and its methods of employment. Divisions usually had only three light or mountain artillery battalions, which were habitually attached to each infantry regiment, an extension of the old concept of positioning artillery directly in the frontline alongside infantry. A medium battalion, if attached, might be kept under division control for counterbattery fire. This means of artillery employment denied the division commander the ability to affect combat power by massing his artillery or providing general support. Artillery preparations prior to an attack were usually short, no more than one or two hours. This included adjustment and ranging, limited counterbattery fire, breeching obstacles (which was of only limited effectiveness with 7.5cm pieces) which meant only about a half-hour's fire on the defenders' frontline positions.

A great deal of emphasis was placed on the employment of infantry crew-served weapons. The LMG formed the core of section and platoon firepower alongside the grenade discharger. The HMG was considered pivotal to the attack by providing suppressive fire through gaps between advancing subunits and to the flanks. It was also essential to defense. While riflemen protected LMGs, LMGs protected HMGs. Infantry guns were extremely light, compact, and simple, and were intended to supplement divisional artillery. Such weapons were found in other armies at regimental level, but the Japanese also allotted them to battalion level in lieu of mortars. Unlike Western armies, in which mortars were organic to companies and battalions, the Japanese employed mortars in non-divisional units for attachment as required. The state of Japanese AT weapons was dismal. The 2cm AT rifle was heavy, cumbersome, and ineffective against all but the lightest Allied tanks. They were few in number too, not all units possessed them. The 3.7cm AT gun was actually a rapid-fire infantry gun designed to knock out pillboxes. With the notable exception of machine guns, the Japanese allocated infantry crew-served weapons on a smaller scale than Western armies.

Small-unit tactics in the Philippines

A number of characteristics of Japanese small-unit tactics were noted in the Philippines. Attacks would often begin at dusk with infiltration through gaps between units and flank attacks. After securing as much ground as possible before complete darkness, they consolidated and prepared defenses for an enemy dawn counterattack. Even though many Japanese battalions had suffered heavy losses during the Bataan assaults, they would strive to keep up pressure on US–Filipino positions, constantly seeking out gaps and weak points. When these were found, they would immediately infiltrate them, to be followed by supporting troops in the hope of establishing a foothold within the US–Filipino position. Harassment of frontline positions was constant with infiltration by individuals and small groups, sniper fire, probes from unexpected directions, and sections frequently opening fire intermittently—all to cause confusion and uncertainty. This was also an effort to draw fire to locate US–Filipino positions. On several occasions the Japanese rapidly occupied abandoned villages and brought in troops by truck, with the result that they received heavy enemy artillery fire. From this they learned to bring troops in through the jungle on foot, and to remain dispersed and concealed.

Japanese artillery tactics were initially ineffective, as they had little experience against an artillery-armed enemy. The camouflage of gun positions was poor and companies were positioned too close together, making them vulnerable to counterbattery fire. They learned quickly though, concealing their guns better and dispersing firing units more widely. They would sometimes employ a single artillery piece to range a target, and then move in a company to accomplish the fire mission; meanwhile the single gun moved to another position, repeated its ranging task for another target, with the company following on quickly to accomplish the next mission.

One American officer commented, "The Japanese are crafty, shrewd, given to deception. They are amazingly patient and wait for hours, even days, for their chance. They are tough individual soldiers and work well in small groups of two or three men."

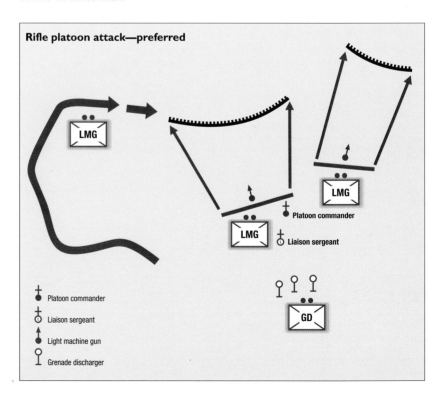

Rifle platoon attack—preferred

LMG

LMG

LMG

Platoon commander

Liaison sergeant

GD

Platoon commander

Liaison sergeant

Light machine gun

Grenade discharger

Weapons and equipment

Japanese individual and infantry crew-served weapons were adequate (with the notable exception of AT weapons), even though they had been developed in the 1920s and 1930s, and sometimes even earlier. They were rugged and fairly reliable, but were comparatively short ranged and did not match the capabilities of contemporary Western weapons in most cases. The short range of infantry weapons was not much of a hindrance in the Pacific though, and the Japanese became adept at employing them offensively and defensively to exploit this characteristic. Their lack of sufficiently heavy and long-range artillery proved to be more of an issue though. This, coupled with outdated fire-control measures, caused them significant problems. Ammunition packaging proved to be inadequate for the extremes of the tropics and was more troublesome than the weapons themselves.

Platoon weapons

Rifles and pistols

The Arisaka 6.5mm Type 38 (1905) and 7.7mm Type 99 (1939) rifles, while heavy and not as finely finished as Western counterparts, were as reliable and rugged as any five-shot bolt-action in service. These rifles had a Mauser-type action stronger than the US M1903 Springfield's. Other versions of the 6.5mm Type 38 included the Types 38 (1905) and 44 (1911) carbines, the latter with a permanently attached folding spike bayonet; Type 38 (1905) short rifle; and Type 97 (1937) sniper rifle with a 2.5x scope. The 7.7mm Type 99 was provided in two lengths, the long rifle for infantry and the short rifle for cavalry, engineers, and other specialty troops (test 7.7mm carbines had too hard a recoil). The long rifle was 50in. in length while the short's was 6in. shorter. Various units within a division carried spare rifles, totaling almost 2,000.

Japanese automatic pistols were of poor quality and lacked knockdown power. The Nambu Type 14 (1925) and the even more poorly designed Type 94 (1934) had eight and six-round magazines, respectively. Both fired an underpowered 8mm cartridge. Rather than being issued as an improvement over the Type 14, the Type 94 was produced only as a lower-cost alternative. Pistols were issued to officers and crew-served weapons' crewmen.

In the mid-1920s, the IJA adopted the bicycle to improve infantry mobility. One battalion in some regiments was equipped with them. Some regiments deployed to Southeast Asia were entirely equipped with bicycles. A bicycle-mounted infantry battalion could average 10–15 mph if necessary, and could carry rations for up to five days. Troops would walk beside their bicycles for a short time each hour to exercise different leg muscles to prolong their endurance.

The core weapon of the Japanese section (squad) was the light machine gun. This 6.5mm Type 96 (1936) LMG is shown with a spare 30-round magazine and a magazine loader/oiler. The 7.7mm Type 99 (1939) was similar in appearance, but had a cone-shaped flash suppressor and a folding monopod butt support. Both were based on the Czechoslovakian Brno design, the same weapon from which the British Bren gun was derived.

Japanese weaponry and equipment designation characters

Character	Meaning
式	Type
一	1
二	2
三	3
四	4
五	5
六	6
七	7
八	8
九	9
十	10

A note on Japanese designations: the terms "type" and "model" were both used to translate the Japanese *Kanji* ideograph *Shik*, which is actually "type." The Japanese ideograph for "model" is *Kata*. Contemporary intelligence documents often used both terms in the same document. "Type" is used throughout this book and "Model" is used for sub-variants.

Machine guns

The Nambu 6.5mm Type 96 (1936) and 7.7mm Type 99 (1939) LMGs were bipod-mounted and fed by 30-round top-fitted magazines. The obsolete Nambu 6.5mm Type 11 (1922) LMG was issued as a substitute to some units and even found alongside the Type 96. It had a unique feed hopper in which 6 five-round rifle charging clips were stacked. This tended to collect dirt and vegetation debris, causing it to jam. Besides its bipod, a tripod was available for the Type 11.

The Japanese had some problems with their LMGs. Their rapid extraction sometimes caused stoppages. To overcome this the Type 11 had a complex oil reservoir, which had to be kept full to oil the cartridges as they were fed. The Type 96 required its cartridges be oiled before loading in the magazine, which was accomplished by an oiler built into the magazine loader. A special reduced-charge round was issued. Standard-load 6.5mm rifle rounds could be used, but with an increased chance of stoppage. The 7.7mm Type 99 was an improved Type 96. It was designed to eliminate the need for lubricated ammunition. Both the types 96 and 99 had 2.5x telescopic sights, quick-change barrels, carrying handles, and little used shield plates. To emphasize the Japanese propensity for close combat, these 20 lb weapons could be fitted with a rifle bayonet.

Japan adopted the 7.7mm round for rifles and LMGs on the eve of the Greater East Asia War, fielding the first weapons in mid-1939. The 6.5mm had performed poorly in China where a longer range, greater power, and more penetration were needed. Divisions and brigades in Japan were the first to be armed with 7.7mm weapons, followed by units in China, then Manchuria and lower priority units in all areas. By the time of the invasion of the south some units deploying from Manchuria still had 6.5mm weapons. It was not uncommon for units deployed to a given area to be armed with different caliber weapons, causing ammunition supply problems.

Grenade dischargers

The 5cm Type 89 (1929) heavy grenade discharger was not only an important close-combat weapon, but was also provided with a full range of colored signal smoke and flares. Besides rifled high explosive (HE) and white phosphorus mortar rounds, the Type 89 could fire hand grenades with a propellant charge fitted. The Type 10 (1921) grenade discharger was still issued as a substitute. Popularly called "knee mortars" by Allied troops due to their curved base plate, these compact weapons could not be fired from the thigh, as was rumored,

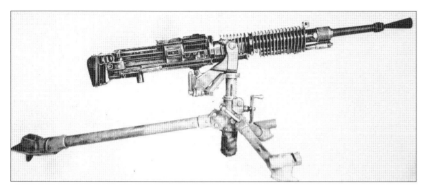

This Nambu 6.5mm Type 3 (1914) HMG equipped battalion machine-gun companies. It was partly replaced by the 7.7mm Type 92 (1932). The two weapons were similar in appearance. The Type 3 had vertical spade grips with large cooling fins on the rear half of the barrel. The Type 92 had two horizontal pistol grips and large cooling fins on only a quarter of the length of the barrel with smaller ones on the rest. Both were based on the French Hotchkiss.

without breaking a leg. Another theory for the source of their nickname is that they were carried in a canvas bag strapped to the thigh—whereas in fact they were carried in a canvas case slung from the shoulder. The Type 100 (1940) rifle grenade launcher was of the cup-type fitting on 6.5mm and 7.7mm rifles. It fired the Type 97 (1937) HE grenade, also the standard hand grenade.

Company/battalion weapons

The battalion machine-gun company was armed with either Nambu 6.5mm Type 3 (1914) or 7.7mm Type 92 (1932) HMGs. Even though these tripod-mounted weapons were fed by 30-round metallic strips, a high rate of fire could be maintained. AA adapters could be fitted to both weapons' tripods and there was a special AA tripod for the Type 3. The 7.7mm HMG used a semi-rimmed cartridge, which could not be fired in rifles and LMGs. The semi-rimmed round had been adopted seven years before the new rifle and LMG round.

Another weapon was the 2cm Type 97 (1937) AT rifle. Capable of semi- and fully-automatic fire with a seven-round magazine, it was surprisingly effective against light tanks and personnel. Its AP-tracer and HE-tracer rounds were not interchangeable with the 2cm machine cannon's. It was heavy, at 150 lbs, and expensive to produce resulting in its limited issue. Units possessing them normally issued them to the battalion gun company, alongside the 7cm infantry gun.

The 7cm Type 92 (1932) battalion infantry gun was issued on the basis of having two in the battalion gun platoon. A few units had a battalion gun company with four pieces. A complex weapon, it nonetheless provided effective direct and indirect fire support. All Japanese infantrymen were issued a Type 30 (1897) bayonet with a 15.75in.-long blade, whether they were armed with a rifle or pistol, or even if they were unarmed.

The 7cm Type 92 (1932) battalion gun was a comparatively compact weapon weighing 468 lbs, and it could be broken down into a half-dozen man- or animal-pack loads. It had a range of 3,060 yds with HE, AT shaped-charge, and illumination rounds. Normally there were no crew-served weapons assigned at company level, but some units did possess company weapons platoons, which may have had a few HMGs and AT rifles. Otherwise, these weapons could be attached to companies from the battalion.

Regimental weapons

The regimental gun company was equipped with the 7.5cm Type 41 (1908) infantry gun (a.k.a. the regimental gun) to provide direct and indirect fire. Comparatively compact and light (1,180 lbs), it could be broken down into six packhorse loads. This weapon was originally adopted as a mountain artillery piece, but when replaced by a new 7.5cm gun in 1934 it was relegated to the infantry-gun role. It was provided HE, shrapnel, armor-piercing high explosive (APHE), AT shaped-charge, and white phosphorus rounds and had a 7,000yd range. The ammunition was not interchangeable with 7.5cm artillery rounds.

The principal Japanese 'antitank' gun was the 3.7cm Type 94 (1934) infantry rapid-fire gun. Originally intended to deliver direct fire to knock out machine guns, it was provided with HE ammunition. Even though an APHE round was issued, it performed poorly as an AT gun owing to its low velocity and poor penetration. It could knock out a US light tank with multiple hits though. Some units deploying from China were armed with more effective 3.7cm Type 97 (1937) AT guns. These were German-made Pak.35/36 guns captured from China.

Artillery

While Japanese artillery pieces were upgraded or replaced by new models between 1925 and 1936, no new designs were fielded after that point. The earlier Japanese artillery pieces were based on German Krupp designs, while the new models were based on the French Schneider. The newer guns had longer barrels, improved velocity, increased elevation and traverse, and split trails rather than box trails; they could be towed by vehicle too, though most were still horse-drawn as towing by vehicle proved to be impractical on Pacific islands and in Southeast Asia jungles. Most still had wooden-spoked wheels.

The 7.5cm Type 94 (1934) mountain gun weighed 1,200 lbs. It equipped half of the 12 divisional artillery regiments committed to the Southern Operations. The metal ammunition containers each held six rounds and weighed 118 lbs when full. A packhorse could carry two containers.

The standard divisional artillery piece was the 7.5cm Type 38 (1905) improved gun. This weapon was an improved version of the original Type 38 in 1915, with barrel trunnions further to the rear for increased elevation, improved equilibrators to counter the heavy barrel, a variable type recoil system, and an open box trail to further increase elevation. Even with these improvements it was still an obsolescent weapon barely adequate for its role. It had a 10,400yd range and could fire 10–12 rounds a minute for short periods. Ammunition included HE, APHE, shrapnel, white phosphorus, chemical, and illumination rounds.

The 7.5cm Type 95 (1935) gun was intended to replace the Type 38, but saw very limited issue. It offered a number of design improvements and a split trail, but only a 1,220yd range advantage. An even less common weapon was the 7.5cm Type 90 (1930). It was a more modern design than the Type 95 and intended for truck-towing, being provided with pneumatic tires. It was mainly issued to independent artillery regiments and tank units. A spoked-wheel version did see limited issue to divisional artillery regiments. It had a longer barrel than other models and was fitted with a muzzle break and long split trails. This gave it a higher muzzle velocity and its wider traverse made it an effective AT weapon. Both the types 95 and 90 used the same ammunition as the Type 38. Many

Most Japanese field artillery was horse-drawn. This 7.5cm field howitzer caisson (left) held 60 rounds, and the limber 40 rounds, and was drawn by six horses.

divisional artillery regiments were armed with the 7.5cm Type 94 (1934) mountain gun. It could be broken down into 11 components for six packhorse loads. While using the same ammunition as other 7.5cm guns, its range was only 9,000 yds.

Japanese "10cm" weapons were actually 105mm weapons. The 10cm Type 91 (1931) howitzer equipped both divisional and independent artillery regiments, although few divisions were provided with a 10cm battalion. It could be found with both pneumatic tires and wooden-spoked wheels. The weapon could fire HE, APHE, shrapnel, and white phosphorus to 11,500 yds at a rate of six to eight rounds a minute. Medium artillery regiments had the 10cm Type 92 (1932) gun. It fired HE, APHE, shrapnel, and white phosphorus to 20,000 yds. It required a different type of ammunition to the 10cm howitzer. This weapon was known for its comparatively long range, making it difficult to detect in hidden jungle positions. On Guadalcanal the Marines dubbed these guns "Pistol Petes." A 10cm mountain howitzer was also available in pack transport form. It only had a 6,000yd range and its HE and illuminating rounds were entirely different to other 10cm ammunition types.

Heavier, non-divisional artillery included the following:

Weapon	Range
12cm Type 38 (1905) howitzer	6,300 yds
15cm Type 38 (1905) howitzer	5,450 yds
15cm Type 4 (1915) howitzer	10,800 yds
15cm Type 96 (1936) howitzer	13,000 yds
15cm Type 89 (1929) gun	27,450 yds
24cm Type 45 (1912) howitzer	15,300 yds
24cm Type 96 (1936) howitzer	15,300 yds
30.5cm Type 7 (1918) short howitzer	13,000 yds
30.5cm Type 7 (1918) long howitzer	16,600 yds
32cm Type 98 (1938) spigot mortar[1]	1,200 yds

Notes:
[1] Often designated 25cm for the spigot diameter; 32cm projectile caliber.

Antiaircraft guns and mortars will be discussed in detail in the second volume in this series, Battle Orders 14: *The Japanese Army in World War II: South Pacific and New Guinea 1942–44*. The principal AA weapons used by the IJA included:

13.2mm Type 93 (1933) machine gun
2cm Type 38 (1938) machine cannon
7.5cm Type 11 (1922) AA gun
7.5cm Type 88 (1928) AA gun
10cm Type 14 (1925) AA gun (actually 105mm)

Mortars included the 8cm (81mm) types 97 (1937) and 99 (1939); 9cm types 94 (1934) and 97 (1937); and 15cm types 93 (1933), 96 (1936) and 97 (1937). With the exception of the 9cm, these were of the common Stokes-Brandt design. These mortars were assigned to non-divisional mortar battalions (see Osprey New Vanguard 54: *Infantry Mortars of World War II*).

The diminutive Type 92 (1932) tankette was armed with a single 7.7mm Type 97 (1937) machine gun (removed here), based on the Czechoslovakian Brno design. It had replaced the 6.5mm Type 91 (1931). Fed by a 30-round magazine, it was the principal tank machine gun. The Type 94 (1934) tankette was identical in design to the Type 92, but had a much larger rear trailing idler wheel, and featured other suspension improvements.

Tanks

Japanese tanks, with most designs dating from the mid-1930s, were inferior to Western models encountered at the beginning of the war. They were very lightly armored, although the armor was of good quality. Their top speed was in the region of 25mph, but the obsolete Type 94 could only manage 20mph. All used diesel engines, but their mobility across rough terrain was somewhat limited. Accommodation was cramped for the medium tank's four-man crew and even more so for the light tank's three-man crew. No periscopes or bulletproof vision blocks were provided, only vision slits, making them vulnerable to small-arms fire. The 3.7cm gun on light tanks was suitable for knocking out pillboxes, as was the 5.7cm on medium tanks. Both were low-velocity weapons and ill suited for engaging enemy tanks. 7.7mm Type 97 (1937) machine guns were mounted in the hull bow and rear of the turret.

The types 92 (1932) and 94 (1934) tankettes were used for reconnaissance, screening, liaison, and hauling supplies to forward positions. They were little use in direct combat. Both had a two-man crew and were sometimes provided with a small 0.75-ton capacity full-tracked trailer for the supply role. Japanese tanks employed in the Southern Operations included the following:

A Type 94 (1934) medium tank emerges from a streambed. This obsolete tank was still in use by the 7th Tank Regiment in the Philippines. The white insignia on the bow identified the regiment's 2d Company. The Type 94 was similar in appearance to the Type 89A and B, but the driver's and bow gunner's positions were reversed.

Type	Armament	Weight
Type 94 (1934) medium tank	5.7cm gun, 2 x 7.7mm MGs	15 tons
Type 97 (1937) medium tank	5.7cm gun, 2 x 7.7mm MGs	15 tons
Type 95 (1935) light tank	3.7cm gun, 2 x 7.7mm MGs	10 tons
Type 92/94 (1932/1934) tankette	1 x 7.7mm MG	3.4 tons

Type 94 (1934) tanks of the Sonoda Detachment churn forward as US–Filipino forces withdraw onto the Bataan Peninsula. The detachment consisted of both of the 14th Army's tank regiments reinforced by a battalion of the 2d Formosa Infantry. A light machine gunner can be seen in the foreground.

Command, control, communications, and intelligence

Command

High command

The Emperor was the Supreme Commander of all Armed Forces. He relied on the Imperial General Headquarters (IGHQ) to execute his will. The Supreme Military Council and the Board of Marshalls and Admirals served as advisors to the Emperor. The IGHQ oversaw the Ministry of War, Army General Staff, Ministry of the Navy, and Navy General Staff plus the Inspector General of Military Training and Inspector General of Army Aviation. General Tojo Hedeki served as the War Minister and Prime Minister. Admiral Shimada Shigetaro was the Navy Minister. The IGHQ was divided into the Army and Navy sections encompassing the ministries of each services and the general staff. General Sugiyama Hajima was the Chief of the Army General Staff.

The Japanese General Staff system was borrowed from the Germans. Graduates of the Army Staff College (*Rikugun Daigakko* or *Rikudai* for short) considered themselves to be elite. Unlike in most armies, the command of a division was not considered the pinnacle of a general officer's career in the IJA. Young general staff officers, identified by a special breast badge, developed tactical plans with which commanders were required to comply (Germany and the USSR used similar systems). Division commanders were more coordinators than true commanders. The key echelon for tactical planning was at army level. Regulations required general staff officers to serve command time, but it was not desirable on their part. General Staff officers were called *Tenposen Guni* (Tenposen Group) after the special badge they wore, which was similar to a large coin of the *Tokugaea* period. Unit officers (*Taizuki Shoko*), who had not attended the Army Staff College, were called

MajGen Edward P. King, Commanding General, Luzon Force, flanked by his staff, discusses surrender terms with Col Nakayama Motoo, 14th Army Operations Officer at the Experimental Farm Station near Lamaon on Bataan's lower south coast.

Muten Guni (non-badge group) and would progress only a limited amount in their careers, outside of good fortune in wartime.

The adoption of the German General Staff system impacted at the highest levels of command. In 1878 the operational and administrative functions of the Army were separated with the former being assigned to the Chief of the General Staff and the latter to the War Minister. This resulted in a unity of command only at the very highest level—the Emperor, as Supreme Commander of both the Army and Navy. This system allowed the Chiefs of the Army and Navy General Staffs direct access to the Emperor (*iaku no joso*), a privilege granted only later to the War and Navy ministers. What this meant was that the Army and Navy were allowed independence of command (*tosuiken no dokuritsu*) from civilian control, namely the War and Navy ministers.

For all practical purposes the operating forces of the IJA were under the direct control of the IGHQ. This included the General Defense Command in the Home Islands, the Kwantung Army in Manchuria, the China Expeditionary Army, and the Southern Army. The Southern Army exercised direct control over the 14th, 15th, 16th, and 25th armies plus a reserve of two divisions and an IMB. A division from the 23d Army would temporarily be under its control to seize Hong Kong. The Guards Division would be detached from the 25th Army to the 15th for initial operations in Thailand then returned to the 25th Army. The 48th Division would be transferred from the 14th Army after the fall of Manila to the 16th Army for use on Java.

Command and staffs

Japanese unit commanders were not assisted by a deputy commander, second-in-command, or executive officer. Only in divisions possessing an infantry group HQ commanded by a major-general could a second-in-command be said to exist. The infantry group commander served as a tactical commander of the collected infantry regiments, but was often detached with a reinforced regiment on independent missions. The formation's chief of staff was the closest thing to a deputy commander, but these were only found at division and higher echelons. At regimental level the operations officer or one of the battalion commanders would be designated to assume command if the commander became a casualty. At battalion level either the adjutant or a company commander would be so designated.

Table 9: unit commanders	
Unit	**Commander/leader**
Section	sergeant
Platoon	lieutenant
Company	captain
Battalion	major
Regiment	colonel[1]
Brigade/Group	major-general
Division	lieutenant-general
Army	lieutenant-general
Area Army	general

Notes:
[1] *Tank, cavalry, reconnaissance, engineer, transport regiments, which were of battalion size, were commanded by a colonel or lieutenant-colonel.*

Japanese staffs were extremely austere by Western standards. Only the division staff possessed formal, specialized staff sections while regiments and battalions had a minimal staff. Additional junior officers seconded from subordinate units or

LtGen Homma Masaharu, Commander, 14th Army, arrives in the Philippines in December 1941. Held responsible for the Bataan Death March, he was shot at Los Baños, Luzon on April 3, 1946 while his subordinates were hung.

overage officers would sometimes augment staffs though. Regimental and battalion staffs have been described already in the *Unit Organization* section.

The division staff consisted of the commander (lieutenant-general), chief of staff (colonel), and adjutant (lieutenant-colonel assisted by a captain and lieutenant) plus a general staff section and an administrative staff section. The general staff section, essentially planners and coordinators, consisted of:

G-1 (lieutenant-colonel)	Operations, training, and communications. Assisted by signal, code, ordnance, and gas officers.
G-2 (major)	Intelligence, maps, censorship, and mobilization.
G-3 (captain)	Rear services, logistics, and lines-of-communication.

The administrative staff section was headed by a lieutenant-colonel, who dealt with reports (except those dealing with operational matters) and oversaw administration. A captain or lieutenant responsible for promotions, appointments, officer and NCO personal records, personnel and mobilization administration; a captain or lieutenant for departmental services and administrative orders; and a captain or lieutenant responsible for documents and secretarial duties assisted him. A small staff of officers, NCOs, and enlisted men assisted all of these officers. There were also five departments in the administrative staff section:

Intendance	A colonel assisted by three lieutenants-colonel or majors, and seven or more captains and lieutenants.
Ordnance	A lieutenant-colonel or major with one or two captains or lieutenants.
Medical	A colonel with two or three medical officers.
Veterinary	A lieutenant-colonel and one or two veterinary officers.
Judicial	A lieutenant-colonel with two or three officers.

Communications

The Japanese relied heavily on field telephones, preferring them to radios. Telephones were more reliable, less expensive, faster to produce, required fewer technical resources, and could be easily issued in large numbers to all echelons. They required little operator training and were more secure from intercept than radios. Japanese field telephones were of the ground return type: that is, they used a single-strand wire and had a metal stake that was driven into the ground and attached to the telephone by a short length of wire. US telephones required a two-strand wire. The standard telephone was the Type 92 (1932) fitted with separate mouth- and earpieces. Field switchboards were provided at battalion and higher echelons to establish party line systems. A lightweight assault field wire was used at regimental and lower levels while a heavier, water-resistant wire was available for semi-permanent systems. Both were covered with yellow braid. At division level and higher, a green, braid-covered, heavy-duty wire was used. A man-carried 600yd wire reel was provided, which could be carried on the back for dispensing wire and on the chest for recovery.

Radios were used in fast-moving offensive situations and when communications had to be established rapidly. Field telephones assumed the primary role during routine action and radio became secondary for standby communications. Japanese radio sets were obsolescent by Western standards. They had wide frequency ranges with plug-in coils to cover the different bands. Tactical field radios used regenerative detectors without frequency amplification. While easy to maintain, it was difficult to keep them on the frequency in use and netted with other sets. The Japanese used amplitude modulated (AM) radios and no frequency modulated (FM) sets. The controls were unusually complex, the sets of marginal construction and poorly waterproofed. The operators, who were highly trained, had to be well versed in radio and antenna theory. Tactical sets were usually 1–50 watts and the transmitters, receivers, batteries, hand

The Type 92 (1932) field telephone weighed 12 lbs. The ground return spike can be seen in front of the set's open front. A Type 95 (1935) telegraph set could be attached to a telephone and used for Morse Code-type administrative traffic. (William Howard Ordnance Technical Intelligence Museum, Largo, Florida)

A radio section in China poses beside its Type 94 (1934) Model 3C radio, a regiment- and division-level set. Radio sections were sizable in order to function 24 hours a day, to be able to man-pack the components if necessary, and to handle the section's three packhorses.

generators, and accessories were carried in separate cases, requiring them to be packed by several men. Most could not be operated while marching, and instead had to be set up. Most could be operated using voice or Morse Code.

The most common tactical sets came from the Type 94 (1934) series. At division and regimental level the Type 94 Model 3 was used; the Type 94 Modesl 5 and 6 were used at battalion and company level. The Model 6 was a "walkie-talkie"-type radio. These radios could also be transported by packhorse.

Another means of communications was the 32-candlepower signal lamp. This set could be man-packed by three men and consisted of a lamp, hand-powered electric generator, and accessories. The light was flashed using a Morse Code-like system and white, green, red, and amber filters. White and other color rectangular and triangular ground-to-air panels were used to signal aircraft and mark positions. Red and white semaphore flags were used, being replaced by blue and yellow flags, respectively, in mist. While the Japanese use thousands of symbols in their written language, the *Kana* alphabet with 48 symbols, each representing a sound in the Japanese language, was used for their Morse Code, semaphore, and light signals. At battalion level and below, extensive use was made of messengers. Limited use was made of messenger dogs and carrier pigeons. At company and lower levels, bugles, whistles, flashlights, and arm signals were used extensively. Colored-smoke projectiles and red, white, and green flares were provided for 5cm grenade dischargers. One- and three-barrel Type 97 (1937) 3.5cm flare pistols were also used. Tank commanders employed an elaborate system of red, red and white, and blue and white triangular pennants for signaling commands and directions. Colored lights were used at night.

Intelligence

The 2d Bureau of the Army General Staff was responsible for intelligence collection, analysis, and dissemination. It was subdivided into the 5th Section (American and European), 6th Section (Asiatic), and the unnumbered Secret Service Section (*Tokumu Kikan*). The 5th and 6th Sections primarily focused on collecting intelligence on American and European (including Australian and New Zealand) forces in the Pacific and not so much on the home countries. There was also a separate 18th Group (Radio Intelligence) in the General Staff. Intelligence was also collected by the Navy General Staff's 3d Bureau and Ministry of Foreign Affairs. Military and naval attachés in Japanese embassies were also instrumental in collecting intelligence.

Overall, Japanese intelligence at the strategic level was inadequate with many higher commanders giving intelligence matters little regard. The Japanese tradition to attack quickly and not consider the situation further undermined the attention given to intelligence by the IJA. However, basic information on the areas of future operations was collected. The order of battle dispositions and armament of military and naval forces was fairly accurate, and a great deal of effort was given to obtaining maps and aerial photographs. There were invariable shortfalls of course; for example, only about a third of northern Luzon in the Philippines had been photographed, but the coverage included the possible landing areas, many of the main highway routes, Manila Bay area, and other key areas. These flights were made in late-1940, so were not entirely up to date. The Bataan Peninsula had not been photographed. Most airfields throughout the Southern Area had been located with very few missed.

Army intelligence agents toured some areas before the war, especially in New Guinea and the NEI. It is known that some of these officers were later assigned to units tasked to seize the areas they had examined. Possible landing areas, approach channels, locations of coast defense guns, and military and naval installations were of primary interest during these tours. Much intelligence was gleaned from signal intercepts of Allied radio traffic, chiefly collected by the IJN. A Unit 82 was established on Formosa before the war to study tropical warfare and disease prevention, but its findings appear to have had little effect on operations.

IJA formations had few tactical intelligence collection assets. Intelligence staffs were small and given low priority. There were only a small number of radio intercept and direction finding units, and these were of modest capability. There were no dedicated ground reconnaissance units above division level. The divisional reconnaissance or cavalry regiment was more of an advance guard and screening unit. Unit patrols were the primary means of collecting battlefield information, but dissemination was slow and limited. Aerial reconnaissance was the most important source of ground force intelligence. Information gained from local natives and sympathizers also proved valuable. In the initial phase of the Pacific War, though, the tempo was fast-paced with the enemy often in disarray and retreating. The Japanese simply steamrollered their way through the countryside and were only concerned with what was immediately in front of them. This no doubt cost the Japanese time and casualties, but they completed most initial operations well within schedule. In fact, this "victory disease" led many officers to believe that staff intelligence sections no longer had a purpose. The Southern Army even eliminated its intelligence section, absorbing part of it into the operations section. This disdain for intelligence efforts was reinforced by the overall contempt the Japanese had for their enemies.

Combat operations

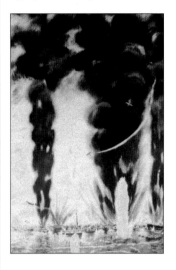

The December 10 air attack on Naval Ammunition Depot, Cavite southwest of Manila created a column of smoke almost 1,000ft high. (Chosei Miwa)

The Commander-in-Chief, Southern Army, shall, in cooperation with the Navy, concentrate his main forces in Indochina, South China, Formosa, and the Ryukyu Islands and shall carry out preparations for the invasion of the strategic southern areas.

Strategic areas to be occupied are the Philippines, British Malaya, the Netherlands East Indies, and a part of southern Burma.

IGHQ High Command record

Limited space only allows a cursory study of the many campaigns and operations in the period and theater under discussion. Many of these operations were complex and involved the commitment of additional forces in later phases. The focus will be on detailing the order of battle of the committed Japanese forces and their basic movements.

Sources, even the Japanese ones, are often in conflict, or incomplete, with regard to the order of battle for specific operations. It was frequent for the designations of minor units not to be included, only their type.

Headquarters, Southern Army remained in Saigon, Indochina through World War II. From there it directed operations across a vast area of operations and coordinated the extensive logistics and shipping efforts. Besides the 14th, 15th, 16th, and 25th armies, the Southern Army was assigned the following units:

Japanese infantrymen in the Philippines make way for their unit's pack train. Draft and packhorses were essential in an army with little motor transport. The machine gunner is armed with the obsolescent 6.5mm Type 11 (1922) LMG. (Ryohei Koiso)

Southern Army units
21st, 56th (-) divisions ⎫
21st IMB ⎬ Reserve
4th IMR ⎭
1st Parachute Force (1st, 2d Raiding regiments)
1st Artillery Command
1st Debarkation Unit
6th, 28th Shipping Engineer regiments
2d Debarkation Unit
10th, 11th, 14th Shipping Engineer regiments
222d, 223d, 224th, 225th Motor Transport regiments

The Philippines

Air attacks on the Philippines were piecemeal and not an overwhelming Pearl Harbor-like attack. The Pearl Harbor attack occurred at 0225, December 8 Philippine time. Notification of the attack was received at 0650. The first IJN air attack struck a seaplane tender in Davao Gulf, Mindanao in the extreme south at 0715, and the first air attacks hit Tuguegarao and Baguio, northern Luzon. Further IJA and IJN attacks on Luzon from Formosa occurred through the day. The major attack on Clark Field arrived at 1130. Devastating attacks on Cavite Navy Yard and Nichols Field were delivered on December 10. Air attacks continued, with IJA aircraft limited north of 16° North and the IJN responsible south of that latitude, a line passing across the south end of Luzon's Lingayen

Gulf. The 14th Army was supported by elements of the 3d Fleet, reinforced by 1st and 2d Fleet elements under Vice Admiral Takanishi Ibo, and the 11th Air Fleet under Vice Admiral Tsukahara Nishizo.

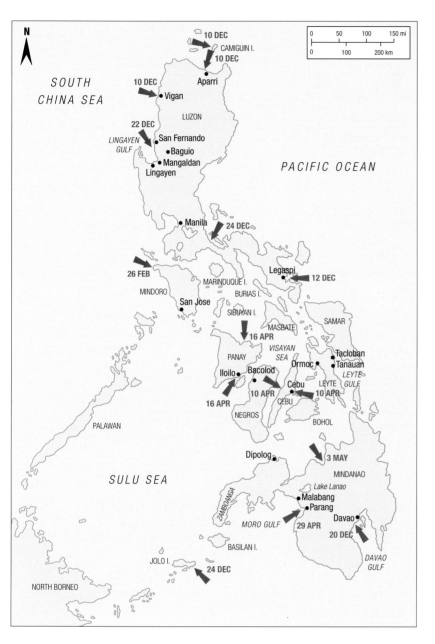

The main Philippine landings, December 10, 1941–May 3, 1942.

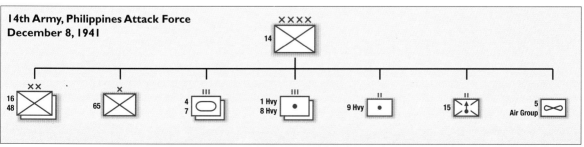

14th Army—Philippines Attack Force
16th Division (14,674)
48th Division (15,663)
65th Brigade (Army Reserve, 6,659)
4th, 7th Tank
14th Signal Regiment
6th Railway Regiment
1st (15cm howitzer), 8th Independent (10cm gun) Heavy Artillery
9th Independent Heavy Artillery Battalion (15cm gun)
15th Independent Mortar Battalion (32cm spigot)
40th, 45th, 47th, 48th Field AA Battalions
30th, 31st Independent Field AA Companies
3d, 21st Independent Engineer
3d Independent Engineer Company
26th, 28th Bridge *Matériel* Companies
13th, 28th River Crossing *Matériel* Companies
1st Field Military Police Unit
1st Sea Operation Unit
Shipping engineer units
Line-of-communications units
38th, 62d, 63d Motor Transport regiments
5th Air Group

In addition to the troops of the divisions and brigade, the 14th Army employed 1,021 men in its HQ, 28,447 in artillery and support units under its direct command, 20,956 line-of-communication troops, and 9,330 shipping engineer troops. Almost 13,000 Air Service personnel participated. There were 10,500 US Army (including Air Force), 12,000 Philippine Scouts (component of the US Army), 1,700 Marines, and 120,000 Philippine Army troops, mostly under US leadership.

Four Advance Attack Forces would land at widely separated sites on Luzon with most launching from Formosa. On December 8 a 490-man Sasebo 2d SNLF, Batan Attack Force, secured tiny Batan Island roughly halfway between Formosa and Luzon. Elements of the IJA 24th Airfield Battalion improved the airstrip and two fighter regiments arrived. An SNLF element then occupied Camiguin Island on the 10th. The same night the Tanka Detachment landed at Aparri on Luzon's north end along with an element at Gonzaga. The Kanno Detachment, led by the II/2 Formosa Infantry commander, landed at Vigan on northwest Luzon. The unopposed landings secured airfields, which were soon operational.

Tanaka Detachment Col Tanaka Toru (2,000)
2d Formosa Infantry (- Kanno Detachment)
1 Battalion (-), 48th Mountain Artillery
40th Field AA Battalion (-)
Airfield service elements

Kanno Detachment LtCol Kanno (2,000)
III Battalion, 2d Formosa Infantry
Two companies, I Battalion, 2d Formosa Infantry
Company, 48th Mountain Artillery
Company, 40th Field AA Battalion
Company, 45th Field AA Battalion
Airfield service elements

On December 12 the Kimura Detachment, detached from 16th Division, from the Palaus landed unopposed at Legaspi on Luzon's southeast Picol Peninsula to secure an airfield for the IJN. This force pushed up the peninsula toward Manila while the Tanaka Detachment, with the Kanno Detachment merged into it after linking up on the 12th, moved south toward Lingayen Gulf leaving small security forces behind.

Kimura Detachment MajGen Kimura Naoki (2,500)
HQ, 16th Infantry Group
33d Infantry (- I Battalion)
Company, 22d FA
Company, 16th Engineer
Kure Ist SNLF 575
Ist Airfield Construction Unit (IJN)

Most of the Advance Force would land on Luzon as the Northern Force, but the Mindanao Invasion Force landed near Davao City on southern Mindanao on December 20 against light resistance. The Sakaguchi Detachment, launched from the Palaus, was actually under 16th Army control, which was responsible for the NEI. The Miura Detachment landed on the north side of Davao and part of the Sakaguchi Detachment to the southwest. The town was seized and the airfield placed in operation. The Miura Detachment, detached from 16th Division and assigned to 14th Army, remained as an occupation force. The bulk of the Sakaguchi Detachment prepared for the British Borneo operation. It quickly dispatched the Matsumoto Detachment to secure Jolo Island halfway between Mindanao and Borneo.

Sakaguchi Detachment MajGen Sakaguchi Shizuo (5,000)
HQ, 56th Infantry Group
Tankette Unit, 56th Infantry Group
Medical Unit
Ist Field Hospital
146th Infantry
I Battalion, 56th FA
Ist Company, 56th Engineer
2d Company, 56th Transport
Miura Detachment Lt Col Miura Toshio
I Battalion, 33d Infantry
2d Kure SNLF
2d Airfield Construction Unit (IJN)

Jolo Island was secured against minimal resistance on December 24 and an airfield established to support the Borneo invasion.

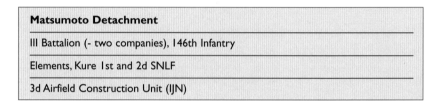

Matsumoto Detachment

III Battalion (- two companies), 146th Infantry

Elements, Kure 1st and 2d SNLF

3d Airfield Construction Unit (IJN)

Luzon operations, December 10, 1941–February 26, 1942.

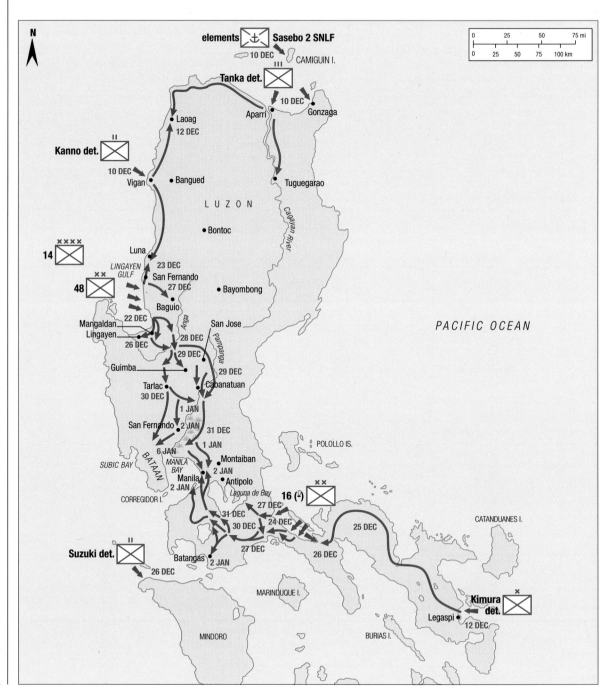

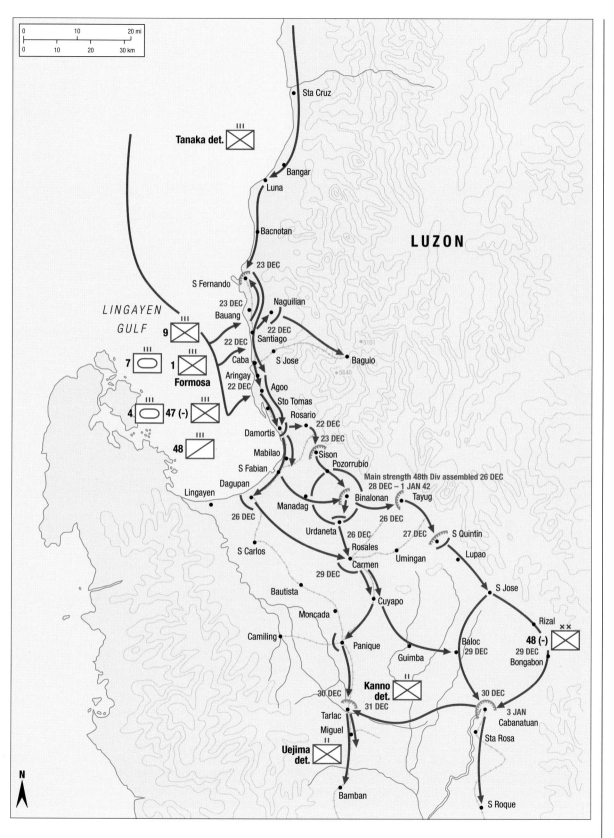

The Lingayen Bay landing, and the drive south to Cabanatuan.

The Main Force for the Luzon landings included the 16th Division assembled at Amami Shima in the Ryukyus and the 48th Division (- Tanaka and Kanno Detachments) was on Formosa and the Pescadores southwest of Formosa. The transports were loaded amid fears of American B-17 bomber attacks and departed on December 17–18. The 84 transports with the 48th Division landed on the east side of Lingayen Gulf just before dawn in a rainstorm on December 22 experiencing light resistance. The 48th Division had somewhat more truck transport than most other divisions and one battalion in each regiment was equipped with bicycles. The much-reinforced Division landed in three echelons.

Lingayen Force

1st Echelon

    47th Infantry (I Battalion)

    4th Tank (- one company)

    48th Reconnaissance

    II Battalion, 48th Mountain Artillery

2d Echelon

    HQ, 14th Army

    HQ, 48th Division

    1st Formosa Infantry

    7th Tank

    Company, 4th Tank

    48th Mountain Artillery (- I and II Battalions)

    48th Engineer (-)

    I Battalion, 9th Infantry (+) (Uejima Detachment)

    1st and 8th Independent Heavy Artillery

    9th Independent Heavy FA Battalion

3d Echelon

    Kamijima Detachment

        II Battalion, 9th Infantry (Army Reserve)

        III Battalion, 9th Infantry (Left Flank Force)

        II Battalion, 22d FA

    14th Signal Regiment

On December 23 the Tanaka Detachment moving from the north linked up with the 48th Division. After fighting a delaying action US–Filipino forces were routed and began a fighting withdrawal toward Bataan Peninsula. The 48th Division drove down the Agno/Pampanga River Valley south to Manila, which was declared an open city on the 27th. The Uejima Detachment (I/9 Infantry) protected the right flank under 14th Army control.

The Lamon Force consisted of 7,000 troops of the 16th Division (- 9th and 33d Infantry). Lamon Bay is located at the northeast side of the neck of the Picol Peninsula where it joins the main island southeast of Manila. The 24 transports departed Amami Shima on December 17 and arrived two days after the Lingayen Force, December 24. Landing in the dark, II/20 Infantry and an artillery company landed at Mauban to secure the right flank and I/20 and the regimental gun company secured the left flank at Siain. The Sasebo 2d

SNLF secured two small islands outside Lamon Bay. US–Filipino forces were withdrawing before the Kimura Detachment pushing up the peninsula and were not prepared to resist the landing. The main body landed near Atimonan and began moving toward Manila. On December 25 the Kimura Detachment linked up with the 16th Division and reverted to its control.

Lamon Force
HQ, 16th Division
20th Infantry (-)
22d Field Artillery (-)
16th Reconnaissance
16th Engineer (-)
Service units

The Japanese focused on Manila, with both the 16th and 48th Divisions racing to the prize. The value of Bataan as a US–Filipino defensive position was not yet realized. With the Japanese pushing from both the north and south toward the capital, the US–Filipino South Luzon Force managed to pass through Manila and reach Bataan while the North Luzon Force conducted a brilliant holding action to keep the road open as the 48th Division pushed to trap the southern force. The tank-heavy Sonoda Force (sometimes referred to as a "tank brigade"), led by the 7th Tank Regiment's commander, spearheaded the effort to cut off the withdrawal along with the reorganized Kanno Detachment to the west, but failed. The South Luzon Force made it through by January 2, 1942. On the same day both 16th and 48th divisions' advance guards entered Manila.

Sonoda Force Col Sonoda Seinosuke
7th and 4th Tank
I Battalion, 2d Formosa Infantry
Company, 48th Engineer

Kanno Detachment LtCol Kanno
III Battalion, 2d Formosa Infantry
Company, 48th Mountain Artillery

After the US–Filipino forces slipped through San Fernando to Bataan the Tanaka Detachment to the east and the Takahashi Detachment to the west continued the pursuit. The Takahashi Detachment was the renamed and reorganized Kamijima Detachment, after its commander had been killed on December 30. A US–Filipino rear guard continued to fight a holding action to allow defenses to be established and the Japanese relieved the battered Tanaka Detachment with the Imai Detachment. The US–Filipino withdrawal into Bataan was completed on January 6. To this point the Japanese had lost only 627 dead and 1,282 wounded. US–Filipino forces had lost 13,000 in combat, to illness, or to desertion.

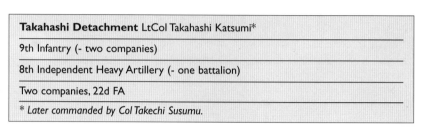

Tanaka Detachment Col Tanaka Toru
2d Formosa Infantry
Company, 7th Tank
Battalion, 48th FA
Battalion, 1st Independent Heavy Artillery
Battalion, 8th Independent Heavy Artillery

Takahashi Detachment LtCol Takahashi Katsumi*
9th Infantry (- two companies)
8th Independent Heavy Artillery (- one battalion)
Two companies, 22d FA
* Later commanded by Col Takechi Susumu.

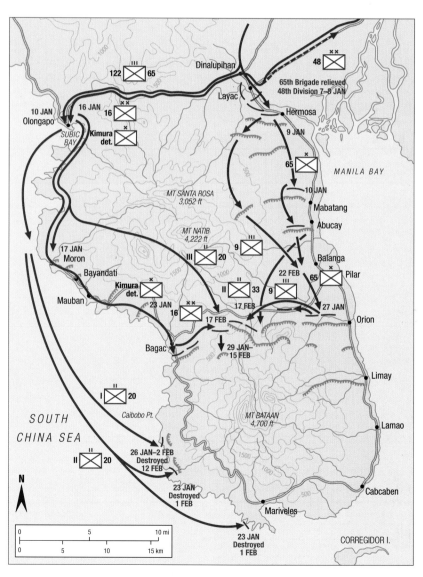

Bataan operations, Phase 1, early-January to late-February 1942. The US–Filipino positions shown (in olive green) are based on Japanese assessments of their deployment, and are not necessarily the same as reported by the Luzon Force.

Imai Detachment Col Imai Hifumi
1st Formosa Infantry
Two battalions, 48th FA
Battalion, 1st Independent Heavy Artillery
Company, 7th Tank

As the 14th Army was preparing to assault Bataan, it received orders to release the 48th Division and 5th Air Group to Java and Thailand, respectively, along with many support units. The 65th Brigade relieved the 48th on January 7–8. Considered a marginal unit with only one month's company-level training, it had landed at Lingayen Gulf on the 1st. Most of the 16th Division has been reassembled, but its 9th Infantry was attached to the 65th Brigade.

Some 80,000 poorly armed, under-supplied US–Filipino troops were now contained on Bataan. The 14th Army attacked on January 9, but after two weeks the attack stalled, even though the enemy suffered heavy losses. The 16th Division

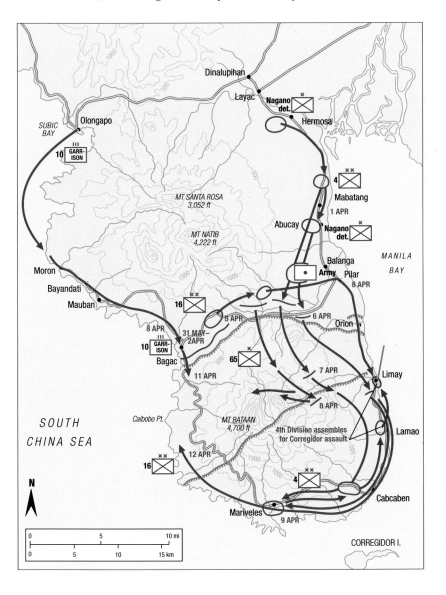

Bataan operations, Phase 2, late-February to early-May 1942. The US/Filipino positions shown are based on Japanese assessments of their deployment, and are not necessarily the same as reported by the Luzon Force.

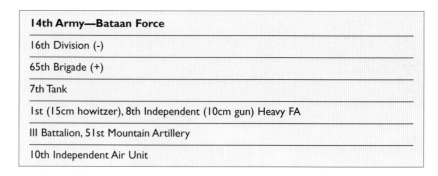

14th Army—Bataan Force
16th Division (-)
65th Brigade (+)
7th Tank
1st (15cm howitzer), 8th Independent (10cm gun) Heavy FA
III Battalion, 51st Mountain Artillery
10th Independent Air Unit

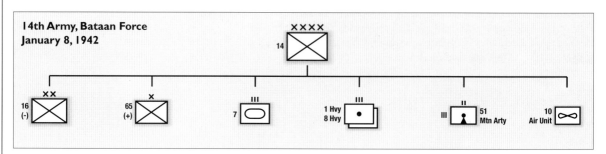

14th Army, Bataan Force
January 8, 1942

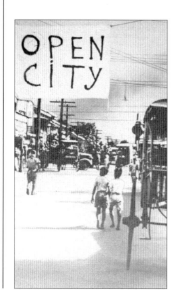

Manila was declared an open city on December 27, 1941 in an effort to halt Japanese bombing, and Japanese internees were released. The advance guards of the 48th Division from the north and 16th Division from the south entered the city on January 2, 1942 to restore order, as widespread looting and arson had broken out.

and Kimura Detachment conducted a holding action on the east coast while the 65th Brigade launched the main attack on the west coast. The III/20 and 9th Infantry conducted attacks in the center. II/20 Infantry landed scattered along Bataan's southwest coast on January 23 and was wiped out by February 1. Next I Battalion landed to the north on the nights of January 26/27 and February 1/2 and was destroyed by February 12. The 9th Infantry, attached to the 65th Brigade, reverted to 16th Division-control on January 31. Exhausted, the Japanese suspended offensive operations on the 8th after losing 7,000 dead and wounded plus 10,000 sick.

Kimura Detachment MajGen Kimura Naoki (5,000)
HQ, 16th Infantry Group
20th Infantry (- 1 Battalion)
122d Infantry, 65th Brigade (- two companies)*
Half gun company, 33d Infantry
AT company, 33d Infantry
* 122d Infantry reverted to 65th Brigade-control on 19 February.

The IGHQ was jubilant over its other successes and was not overly concerned that Bataan was behind schedule. The IGHQ Reserve, the 4th Division, was dispatched from Shanghai. It was poorly equipped and undermanned with only 10,957 troops. Its battalions had only three companies, no AT guns, and it lacked two of its four hospitals. Three reinforced regiments detached from other divisions along with numerous artillery units from Malaya and Hong Kong were sent. Some 7,000 replacements for the battered 16th Division and 65th Brigade also arrived. The reinforcements arrived between mid-February and early-April.

The renewed offensive began with preliminary operations on March 12. On April 3 the main assault began with the 16th Division in the west conducting a diversionary attack while the 4th Division and the Nagano Detachment broke through in the east. The 65th Brigade penetrated the center resulting in a general US–Filipino retreat. The 10th Independent Garrison Unit (10 Dokuritsu Shubitai)

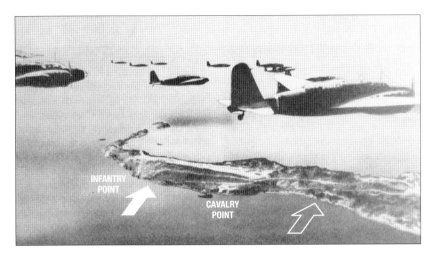

INFANTRY POINT

CAVALRY POINT

IJN Type 97 (1937) Model 2b "Sally" bombers approach Corregidor. The white strip on the island's tail is Kindley Landing Field. The 61st Infantry's planned landing site was to the right of Cavalry Point, but the actual landing was between Cavalry and Infantry points.

Nagano Detachment (21st Division) (3,939)

HQ, 21st Infantry Group, MajGen Nagano Kameichiro

62d Infantry

    Battalion, 51st Mountain Artillery

    Company, 21st Engineer

Kawaguchi Detachment (18th Division) (3,622)

HQ, 35th Infantry Brigade, MajGen Kawaguchi Kiyotake

124th Infantry

Kawamura Detachment (5th Division) (2,667)

HQ, 9th Infantry Brigade, Kawamura Sburo

41st Infantry

Ikuta Detachment

10th Independent Garrison Unit, Col Ikuta Torao

    31st–35th Garrison battalions

61st Infantry troops are shown here disembarking from landing boats on Corregidor's north coast, in what is probably either a staged photograph or one showing late-arriving troops. So many landing craft were lost during the first assault that the 37th Infantry's follow-on assault could not be delivered to the island's west end, denying the Japanese their typical double-envelopment landing.

The assault on Corregidor, May 5–6, 1942.

A unit pack train passes through a Filipino village. It was common for horse-handlers to make straw "sun bonnets" to protect their charges from the heat. (Yoshinobu Sakakura)

Final US line
Gun battery
AA battery
12" mortar battery
Japanese attacks

MANILA BAY

BATAAN PENINSULA

Cabcaben
Mariveles

Caballo Is. (Fort Hughes)
El Fraile Is. (Fort Drum)
Ternate
Calumpan

Corregidor Is. (Fort Mills)
Carabao Is. (Fort Frank)

CHINA SEA

Actual landing 5 May 42
North Pt.
Kindley Landing Strip
Monkey Pt.

4 Div
61
EAST SECTOR

Cavalry Pt.
Planned landing

AA
DENVER

KYSOR
Infantry Pt.

Artillery Pt.
6 May 42
4
3 1

Engineer Pt.
MALINTA HILL
South Dock
San Jose
4
4
Res
Reserve area
2 3

BOTTOMSIDE
North Dock
STOCKADE
RAMSAY RAVINE
RAMSAY
GOVERNMENT RAVINE
CROCKETT
Geary Pt.

MIDDLE SECTOR
4 Div
37
3 1
Cancelled landing
Battery Pt.

MIDDLESIDE
MORRISON HILL
TOPSIDE
Officers Quarters
Golf Course
GEARY
12

Morrison Pt.
MORRISON
JAMES
2 3
JAMES RAVINE

Hospital
Topside Barracks
Parade Ground
WAY
12
WHEELER

WEST SECTOR
GRUBBS
HEARN
SMITH
CHENEY
MONJA
CHENEY RAVINE

Rockey Pt.

N

0 200 400 600 800 1000 m
0 200 400 600 800 1000 yds

1st Artillery Command LtGen Kitajima Kishio
5th Artillery Intelligence Regiment
1st Heavy FA (24cm howitzer)
3d Independent Mountain Artillery
9th Independent Heavy Artillery Battalion (15cm gun)
2d (15cm), 14th (32cm spigot) Independent Heavy Mortar Battalion
3d Mortar Battalion
20th Independent Mountain Artillery Battalion
2d Independent Heavy Artillery Company (15cm gun, 24cm howitzer)
Company, 21st Heavy Artillery (15cm howitzer)
3d Tractor Unit
1st Observation Balloon Company*
23d Independent Engineer
Company, 26th Independent Engineer
* This company's balloon was positioned north of Bataan out of artillery range to observe its north end.

Troops of the 61st Infantry fight their way up what they nicknamed "Gun Smoke Road," located on Corregidor's "tail," heading toward Malinta Hill and the tunnel complex housing the island's command post. The fire-swept road was littered with wrecked vehicles after months of bombardment. (Genichiro Inokuma)

relieved the 16th Division as it shifted to the east and followed the 4th Division around the south end to mop up the east coast. After a hard fight and existing on starvation rations some 75,000 US–Filipino troops surrendered on April 9. Now 10,260 US–Filipino troops held out on Corregidor and other Manila Bay fortified islands. The 4th Marines was responsible for "The Rock's" beach defenses.

Corregidor was pounded by bombers from December 29, 1941 until January 6. Occasional raids were launched and artillery bombardment commenced on February 5 followed by renewed air attacks on March 24. More heavy artillery joined in after Bataan fell to total 116 pieces (7.5, 10, 15, 24cm). The Nagano Detachment had been assigned the assault, but it was reassigned to the 4th Division and set for May 5. The assault force departed Bataan in darkness and was heavily battered by Corregidor's coast defense guns. I and II/61 Infantry landed on the north shore of the island's eastern tail and fought toward the larger west end. The 37th Infantry was unable to conduct the follow-on landing on the west end, as so many landing barges were lost in the first landings. The garrison surrendered the next morning. The other three fortified islands surrendered to the 33d Infantry the next day. Japanese losses were heavy, not only on Corregidor,

LtGen Jonathan M. Wainwright, Commanding General, US Forces in the Philippines, discusses terms of surrender with LtGen Homma Masaharu, Commander, 14th Army on Bataan, on May 6, 1942. Wainwright could only surrender those forces on Corregidor and the other Manila Bay fortified islands, and not those in the southern Philippines. Homma left the meeting and Wainwright returned to Corregidor, where he surrendered to Col Sato Gempachi, Commander, 61st Infantry. (Saburo Miyamoto)

but on Bataan as well. The 5th and 16th Divisions and 65th Brigade were no longer effective fighting units. The 2,690-man 20th Infantry had ceased to exist.

Corregidor Landing Force (4th Division)
Corregidor Left Flank Force
61st Infantry Col Sato
Platoon, 7th Tank *
Battery, 51st Mountain Artillery
1st Company, ? Independent Mortar Battalion
Corregidor Right Flank Force
HQ, 4th Infantry Group MajGen Taniguchi Kureo
37th Infantry Col Koura Jiro
Battalion, 8th Infantry (+)
Elements, 4th and 23d Independent Engineer
Element, 1st Sea Operation Unit (80 landing barges)
Service elements
South Flank Force
33d Infantry, 16th Division
* Four medium tanks (two lost), one captured M3.

While the battles for Bataan and Corregidor raged, southern Luzon was occupied by only Col Suzuki Tatsunoshke's 33d Infantry (- I and II Battalions) and the 16th Reconnaissance (- one company). Its primary mission was to prevent Filipinos sending food to Corregidor from Manila Bay's south shore. A new Suzuki Detachment (III/33 Infantry; company, 22d FA) was organized and on February 26 it landed unopposed on the north end of Mindoro southwest of Luzon. There were only 50 defenders in the south. Further operations to occupy the Visayas, the many islands in the central Philippines, and the south began in April. The 65th Brigade moved to north Luzon for occupation duty.

The Kawaguchi Detachment on Borneo (detached from the 18th Division in Malaya) landed on Cebu on April 10. The main landing was on the west-central coast and at five other points to include the east coast. The 6,500 defenders were pushed into the hills and the Japanese declared the island secure on the 19th.

Panay, defended by 7,000 US–Filipino troops, was next. The 5th Division had sent the Kawamura Detachment from Thailand. It landed on the north and south ends on April 16. A smaller element landed on the west coast on the 18th. The defenders quickly withdrew into the hills and the island was declared secure on the 20th.

While the south coast of Mindanao had been secured in late December, significant US–Filipino forces were still at large on the Philippines' second largest island. The Kawaguchi Detachment, after securing Cebu, landed on the west-central coast of Mindanao on April 29. The Miura Detachment, from the original invasion force, moved west from Davao Bay. The 32d Naval Base Force landed on the north coast on March 2 while the Kawamura Detachment from Panay also landed in the north the next day. After sharp engagements the US–Filipino force surrendered on May 10. The Nagano Detachment, after fighting on Bataan, occupied Negros, Bohol, Leyte, and Samar between May 20 and 25. Only small US–Filipino forces defended these islands.

After the surrender of Corregidor there was confusion as to the surrender of US–Filipino forces in the central and southern Philippines. MacArthur attempted to counter Wainwright's order for those forces to surrender. Fearing the captives held on Luzon would be massacred, the southern forces formally surrendered between May 10 and 26 with the last elements surrendering on June 9. Only very small numbers on these islands actually surrendered with most withdrawing into the hills and organizing guerrilla operations. The Japanese only occupied the cities and a few larger towns, seldom venturing into the countryside except in large bodies in unenthusiastic efforts to engage the guerrillas. Some 10,000 Japanese died in the Philippines. Not crippling for a force of 142,000 (exclusive of the IJN), but by far the highest losses suffered in the Southern Operations and the combat units had to be rebuilt, some twice.

On June 29 the 14th Army was relieved from Southern Army control and placed directly under the IGHQ. LtGen Homma was recalled to Japan and given a victor's welcome, but was not allowed to deliver his report directly to the Emperor. Considered disgraced for failing to continue the attack on Bataan without reinforcement and for not meeting the time schedule, he was relieved by LtGen Tanaka Shizuichi and placed on the reserve list in August 1943.

Netherlands East Indies

The conquest of the NEI was a complex and lengthy operation. Widely scattered Royal Netherlands East Indies Army, British and Australian units, and even a single US artillery battalion defended the vast chain of islands. Only on Java were significant Allied forces concentrated. The American-British-Dutch, Australia Command (ABDACOM) was established to defend the "Malay Barrier," but the forces were too diverse, scattered, weak, and uncoordinated to be effective. When the Netherlands fell to Germany on 15 May 1940 the NEI remained autonomous. Vichy France agreed to place the NEI under Japanese and French "protection," which of course was rejected by the NEI government. The NEI suspended all exports to Japan, which was demanding more oil in light of the US and Commonwealth embargo.

The first Dutch territory seized by Japan were the tiny Tamelan Islands between Borneo and Singapore. A naval landing party came ashore on December 27. The five-prong campaign was launched on January 11, 1942 once operations were well underway in Malaya, Thailand, and Burma. The NEI operation would be conducted in several phases. Initially the 16th Army committed only the 2d Division and 35th and 56th Infantry Groups (aka 56th Mixed Infantry Group) detached from the 56th Division. The 38th and 48th Divisions would be committed later. The 2d Fleet supported the NEI operations.

The first operations were actually aimed at British Borneo, the northern third of the island and included North Borneo and two British protectorates, Sarawak and Brunei, plus Labuan Island at the mouth of Brunei Bay, one of the British Straits Settlements. Both British and Dutch Borneo were coveted for their oil and rubber.

The Kawaguchi Detachment, detailed from the 18th Division in China (now in Malaya), was assigned to seize British Borneo. It departed Cam Ranh Bay, Indochina on December 12. In darkness on the 16th the Right Flank Unit (124th Infantry [-]) landed unopposed at Miri and the Left Flank Unit (III/124) at Seria, Brunei. The oilfields and airfields were to be captured and placed in operation as

A heavy machine-gun crew moves forward. In the East Indies the few roads were often obstructed by Allied roadblocks and prone to air attacks. The jungle was dense and trails few. The infantry would simply use streams as trails, making faster headway than cutting through the jungle would achieve.

16th Army—East Indies Attack Force
2d Division
35th Infantry Brigade
56th Infantry Group
17th Independent FA
1st Independent Engineer
39th, 109th Motor Transport Regiments

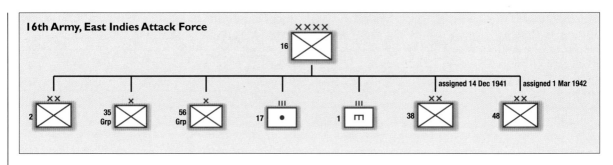

16th Army, East Indies Attack Force

Borneo operations, December 12, 1941–February 13, 1942.

soon as possible. The defenders had destroyed most facilities though. III/124 Infantry landed from small boats at Sandakan, North Borneo on the 19th. Despite Allied air attacks, I and II/124 re-embarked their transports and landed at Kuching, Sarawak on the 22nd. The defending Indian battalion suffered heavy losses and was forced to retreat into northwest Dutch Borneo. The Japanese progressively occupied every major town on British Borneo. They suffered few losses and the Indian battalion was forced to surrender on April 1.

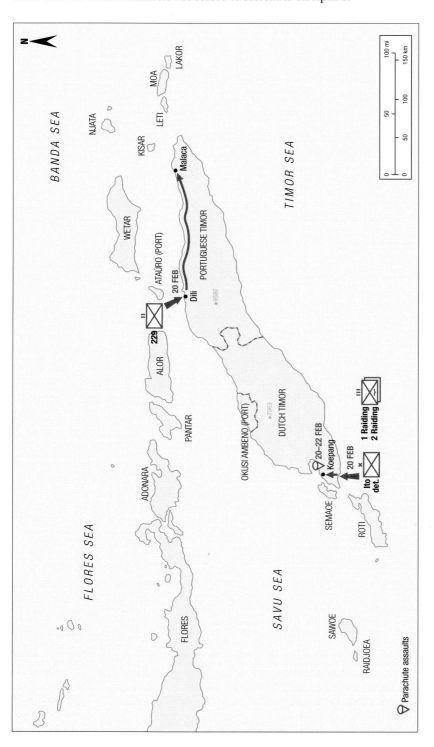

Timor operations, February 1942. The Ito detachment occupied Koepang, Dili, and Malaca. It was relieved by the 48th Division between October and December 1942.

Kawaguchi Detachment MajGen Kawaguchi Kiyotake
HQ, 35th Infantry Brigade
124th Infantry (3,275)
Company (- two platoons), 26th Independent Engineer
Platoon, 12th Engineer
Elements, 18th Division Signal Unit
Elements, 18th Division Medical Unit
4th Field Hospital
Element, 11th Water Supply Unit
33d Field AA Battalion
2d Independent Engineer Company
80th Independent Radio Platoon
37th Fixed Radio Unit
Element, Oil Drilling Section, 21st Field Ordnance Depot
1st–4th Field Well Drilling Companies
HQ, 48th Anchorage
118th Land Duty Company
Element, Yokosuka 2d SNLF 746
4th Naval Construction Unit 260

The Sakaguchi Detachment seized Tarakan Island on the upper east coast of Dutch Borneo on 11 January. The unit was sent from Mindanao in the Philippines to land on the small island's east coast. After stout resistance the 1,300 Dutch surrendered the next day, the day on which Japan finally declared war on the NEI.

Sakaguchi Detachment MajGen Sakaguchi Shizuo (5,500)
HQ, 56th Infantry Group
Tankette Company, 56th Infantry Group
Group Medical Unit (with 1st Field Hospital)
146th Infantry
1 Battalion, 56th FA
1st Company, 56th Engineer
2d Company, 56th Transport
Element, Kure 2d SNLF
2d Oilfield Construction Unit (IJN)
5th Airfield Construction Unit (IJN)

Following Tarakan, the Sakaguchi Detachment reorganized to assault Balikpapan and its important oilfields. On 20 January the convoy departed Tarakan and arrived at Balikpapan on the night of the 24th. American destroyers sank six transports, but the troops had already loaded aboard their landing craft. The main body, the Attack Unit, landed north of Balikpapan reaching the outskirts on the 25th. A detached battalion, the Surprise Attack Unit, infiltrated up a river south of the town and then moved north to Balikpapan. The two units occupied the town on the 26th after moderate fighting.

The Kume Detachment with I/146 Infantry (- two companies) was then formed to secure the major airfields. A detachment of the 146th Infantry was shipped south and moved overland to seize Bandjermasin on Borneo's south

Sakaguchi Detachment

HQ, 56th Infantry Group
Assault Unit, Col Yamamoto
146th Infantry (- II Battalion, - two companies)
I Battalion, 56th FA
1st Company, 56th Engineer (- platoon)
Armored Car Company, 56th Reconnaissance
Surprise Attack Unit Maj Kaneuji
II Battalion, 146th Infantry
Platoon, 1st Company, 56th Engineer
Independent engineer platoon
Salvage Unit Maj Takagi
Field AA battalion
Two companies, 146th Infantry
Independent engineer company (- platoon)
Transport company
Two radio platoons
Group Medical Unit
Company, Kure 2d SNLF

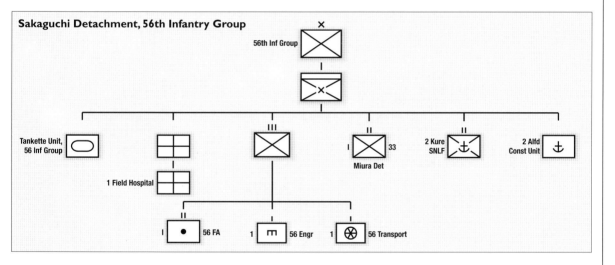

Sakaguchi Detachment, 56th Infantry Group

end, which accomplished its mission on February 13. A battalion of the 124th Infantry, dispatched from Sarawak, occupied Pemangkat on Dutch Borneo's upper west coast on 27 January and then Pontianak, defended by 500 Dutch, to the south, on the 29th.

Celebes was garrisoned by 3,100 Dutch troops in three remote locations. The IJN seized this sprawling island with the 3,500-man Sasebo Combined SNLF (Sasebo 1st and 2d SNLFs) landing on the north peninsula on January 11. The Yokosuka 1st SNLF, staging from Davao, Mindanao, parachuted onto Menado Airfield on the same peninsula. Elements of the Kure 1st SNLF landed on the southeast peninsula on the 24th. On February 9 troops of the Sasebo Combined SNLF landed at Makassar to overwhelm the defenders, all of whom surrendered by the month's end.

Ambon is a small island off the south coast of Ceram. Its occupation was necessary to secure airbases to cover the Banda Sea gap between Timor. This was a main approach into the NEI from Australia. The Ito Detachment was dispatched from the 38th Division after having seized Hong Kong. The SNLF was sent from Davao. 2,800 NEI troops and a reinforced Australian battalion of 1,170 defended the island. The defenders were on the Laitimor Peninsula jutting from the south coast. On the night of January 30/31 the SNLFlanded at the isthmus joining the peninsula to the main island and the Ito Detachment on the southeast end. The Dutch forces surrendered on January 31 and the Australians on February 1.

Timor was divided in half between Dutch (west) and Portuguese (east) Timor. Dutch Timor was defended by 600 Dutch and 1,320 Australian troops. Neutral

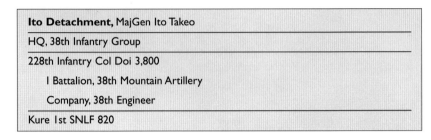

Ito Detachment, MajGen Ito Takeo
HQ, 38th Infantry Group
228th Infantry Col Doi 3,800
I Battalion, 38th Mountain Artillery
Company, 38th Engineer
Kure 1st SNLF 820

Sumatra operations, February 6–March 17, 1942.

Portuguese Timor was garrisoned by 400 colonial troops when 320 Australian commandos and 260 Dutch troops occupied the colony's capital, Dili. The Portuguese governor protested as he had the option of requesting assistance from the Australians and Dutch if attacked by Japan, but this had not yet occurred. A Portuguese battalion was en route from Mozambique, Africa, but it would turn back when the Japanese landed at Dili. The Ito Detachment and

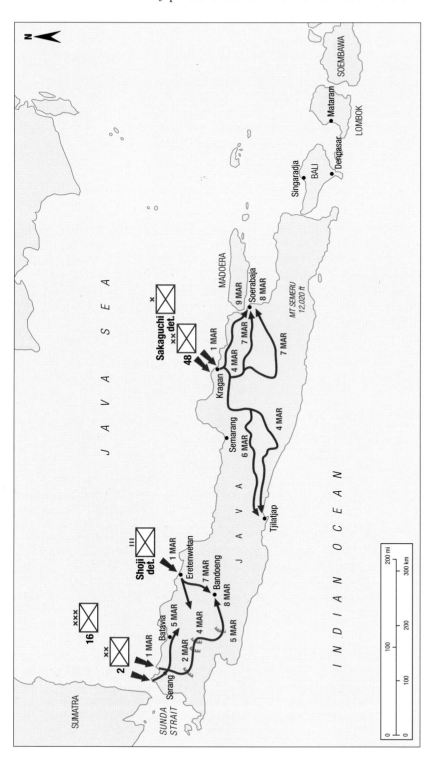

300 men of the Yokosuka 3d SNLF landed on February 20 on Dutch Timor's south coast behind the defenders. Some 350 paratroopers of the 1st and 2d Raiding Regiments parachuted onto airfields with 700 more dropped over the next two days. On February 20 Japanese troops detached from the 229th Infantry, possibly a battalion, landed near Dili disregarding Portugal's neutrality. The Australians withdrew into Portuguese Timor on the 24th, the 250 survivors later linking up with the commando company. They began a successful guerrilla war aided by the Dutch, Portuguese, and Timorese on East Timor first tying down the Ito Detachment and later the entire relieving 48th Division.

The 25th Army was responsible for Malaya and was also assigned Sumatra even though the 16th Army was responsible for the rest of the NEI, due to Sumatra's proximity to Malaya. The second largest concentration of NEI troops defended Sumatra with 4,500 men plus a few thousand Australian and British personnel were on the island, mainly aircrews and service personnel. More Commonwealth troops would arrive after Singapore fell on February 15. At the same time Australian and British ground combat units arrived. The conquest of Sumatra would be conducted in two phases although air battles were being fought over the island as the Malayan campaign intensified.

On 14 February 260 paratroopers of the 1st Raiding Regiment, staging from Malaya, dropped onto an airfield and oil refineries at Palembang on southeast Sumatra. They were reinforced by more over the next couple of days. The island capital, Palembang, soon fell on the 15th. The 38th Division at Cam Ranh Bay, Indochina, was assigned Sumatra having been relieved from 23d Army, under which it seized Hong Kong. A battalion of the 229th Infantry secured Banka Island off the coast from Palembang on the 14th. On the 15th the rest of the 229th Infantry, reinforced by III/230 Infantry, and under the command of Col Tanaka, moved up the Musi River by landing barge to assault Palembang. This force soon entered the capital. On the 17th some 3,000 Commonwealth and Dutch troops were evacuated across the Sunda Strait to Java after abandoning much equipment. On the 23rd the Japanese incited a native uprising on northern Sumatra. Most of southern Sumatra was secured by the 24th with significant numbers of defenders and evacuees from Singapore surrendering.

The second phase of securing Sumatra began on March 12 when the Guards Division arrived from Singapore. Elements of the Division landed at Madan on the upper northeast coast and Koetaradja on Sumatra's northeast end as well as other sites experiencing little resistance. A force from the 38th Division in the south later linked up with the Guards Division. Fort de Koch was secured on the 17th and on the 28th the remaining 2,000 Dutch troops surrendered.

The NEI's main and most populated island was Java with 43 million. Batavia, near the north end, was the capital of both the NEI and Java. Three Dutch "divisions," large brigades, defended the island with 9,000 Dutch regulars, 14,000 Dutch volunteers, and 126,000 native troops. 3,500 British and 3,000 Australian troops plus a US artillery battalion backed these. There were also some 12,000 British and Dutch air force personnel. The main naval base in the NEI was located at Soerabaja on the eastern north coast.

With Sumatra to the northwest mostly secured by the Japanese, the small island of Bali off Java's east end was then seized to begin the larger island's isolation. The 2,000-man Kanemura Detachment from the 48th Division, with III Battalion, 1st Formosa Infantry, landed unopposed on Bali's south coast on February 19 securing the island the next day. Allied naval forces attempted to intercept the invasion force during the Battle of Badoeng Strait off Bali's east end, but the Japanese prevailed. With Sumatra in Japanese hands and the Allies uncertain that Java could be held, ABDACOM was dissolved on February 25. Two Japanese convoys were approaching Java and most remaining Allied ships attempted to intercept the eastern force. The resulting Battle of the Java Sea on the 27th saw the surviving Allied ships fleeing around Java's west end where more were lost during the Battle of Sunda Strait on the 28th. Allied sea and air power in the area were now virtually non-existent. A two-prong attack, west and east, would be directed at Java.

While the landings met light resistance, the Allied counterattacks and delaying actions inflicted some damage on the 2d Division as the three detachments pushed south and east toward inland Bandoeng with the Nasu Detachment in the lead. By the 5th all Allied units had withdrawn to Bandoeng.

Nasu Detachment MajGen Nasu Yumio
HQ, 2d Infantry Group
16th Infantry (- I Battalion)
I Battalion, 2d FA (- 1st Company)
1st Company, 2d Engineer
Two truck transport companies
2d Reconnaissance (attached after landing)

Fukushima Detachment Col Fukushima Kyusaku
4th Infantry (- III Battalion)
II Battalion, 2d FA
5th Independent AT Battalion
2d Company, 2d Engineer

Sato Detachment Col Sato Hanshichi
29th Infantry
2d Tank
1st Company, 2d FA
2d Engineer (- two companies)

With the 2d Division landing on Java's northwest end, a force was needed to land to the east to secure the flank and cut off Allied forces from the eastern portion of the island. The Shoji Detachment was detached from the 38th Division, which had taken Hong Kong and was preparing for Sumatra, and attached to 16th Army on January 16. The Detachment itself was at Hong Kong, moved to Formosa, then Cam Ranh Bay. It had departed the same time as the 2d Division, but took a separate route to land well east of Batavia at Eretanwetan and seized an inland airfield. After inflicting heavy casualties on the British it moved west toward Bandoeng. At one point though a 1st Dutch Division counterattack forced it to withdraw from Soebang, but it soon regained the lost ground.

Shoji Detachment Col Shoji Toshishige
230th Infantry (- III Battalion)
Battalion, 38th Mountain Artillery (- one company)

(continued on page 82)

Company, 38th Engineer (- two platoons)
Independent AT battalion (- two companies)
Light tank company
Field AA company
Two independent engineer companies (each - one platoon)
Platoon, bridge *matériel* company
Truck transport company
Element, airfield battalion
Element, HQ, 40th Anchorage

The 2d Division continued to close in on Bandoeng from the west and north as the Shoji Detachment approached from the east. The Sakaguchi Detachment also moving in from the east would cut off escape to the south (see below). NEI native troops were demoralized and deserting, Allied aircraft had been destroyed or evacuated, and there was no hope of reinforcement or evacuation. The Dutch commander surrendered 66,250 troops on 8 March and the Japanese claimed victory in western Java the next day. It was determined that a guerrilla war would be impractical considering the animosity of many Indonesians towards Westerns. On the 12th 5,600 British, 2,800 Australians, and 900 Americans surrendered.

The 48th Division had been withdrawn from the Philippines at the end of January and concentrated on Jolo in the Sulu Archipelago to prepare for eastern Java operations. Its convoy departed on February 19 calling at Balikpapan, Borneo to embark the Sakaguchi Detachment from the 56th Division (less the detachment which had captured Bandjermasin). The convoy departed on the 23rd, but was attacked by Allied aircraft en route. This delayed the landing by 24 hours and the convoy arrived off eastern Java on 1 March. The 48th Division landed at Kragan west of Soerabaja that morning. The Imai Unit landed west of Kragan to secure the right flank and provide artillery support. The Abe Unit landed to the east of the town to protect the Tanaka Unit as it seized the Tjepoe Oilfield. The Tanaka Unit would then secure Bodjonegoro inland along with the Kitamura Unit (aka Bodjonegoro Raiding Unit) under LtCol Kitamura Kuro, consisting of the 48th Reconnaissance. All units, after moving well inland, then advanced on Soerabaja from the south. The Sakaguchi Detachment separated from the main force and moved west to occupy Tjilatjap on the south coast blocking the evacuation of Allied forces concentrated at Bandoeng. As elsewhere the Dutch fought a delaying action falling back on Soerabaja. They were successful in holding back the Japanese until the 8th when the invaders finally entered the city. Most Allied forces had withdrawn to Madoera Island just off of Soerabaja, but surrendered on the 9th. The area was declared secure on the 12th.

Imai Unit (Right Wing Unit) Col Imai Hifumi
1st Formosa Infantry (- III Battalion)
III Battalion, 48th Mountain Artillery
Company, 48th Engineer

With Java secured, the Sakaguchi Detachment returned to Burma rejoining the 56th Division. The Kanemura Detachment on Bali rejoined the 48th Division on Java while the IJN took over responsibility for Bali and the Lesser Sunda Islands east of Java. The Shoji Detachment on Java was moved to Sumatra

Abe Unit (Left Wing Unit) MajGen Abe Koichi
HQ, 48th Infantry Group
47th Infantry
Battalion, 48th Mountain Artillery
Company, 48th Engineer

Tanaka Unit (aka Tjepoe Raiding Unit) Col Tanaka Tohru
2d Formosa Infantry
Battalion, 48th Mountain Artillery
Company, 48th Engineer

Sakaguchi Detachment Maj Gen Sakaguchi Shizuo
HQ, 56th Infantry Group
146th Infantry (-)
I Battalion, 56th FA
1st Company, 56th Engineer
2d Company, 56th Transport Regiment
Group Medical Unit

to rejoin the 38th Division and the units on Timor also deployed to Sumatra with the 48th Division taking over occupation duties on Timor. The 2d Division garrisoned Java.

South Seas

The Japanese had controlled the Mandated Territory since 1920 having taken it from Germany in 1914. This vast area of the Central Pacific encompassed the Marshall, Caroline, and Mariana Islands. The Mandate, granted by the League of Nations, had given Japan full control of over 2,000 small islands. Only Guam on the south end of the Marianas, an American possession since 1899, was outside their span of control. To defend the Mandates the 4th Fleet was established in 1939 from the South Sea Defense Force. After serving a two-year notice Japan withdrew from the League of Nations in 1935 and the Mandate was closed to Westerners. Japan established a self-contained defense system in each of the three island groups centered on Jaluit, Truk, and Saipan, respectively. Truk was developed as Japan's equivalent of Pearl Harbor. As late as 1939 Japan denied it was fortifying the islands.

The 4th Fleet was not an operational fleet in the normal sense, but contained amphibious, light forces, and air forces to defend the Mandate. It was assigned a limited offensive mission to support the Pacific War though. It was given the task designation of the South Seas Force and charged "To occupy Wake Island; defend and patrol the inner South Seas area and protect surface traffic; cooperate with the Army in the successive occupation of Guam and Rabaul." It would also seize British possessions in the Gilbert Islands to the south and then expand into the Solomons. Further offensive operations would be launched from there to cut off the Southern Lifeline between the US and Australia and New Zealand.

Initially only a single IJA unit would participate in these operations. The Z Operation was planned to commence on December 8. The Guam invasion force was the South Seas Detachment (*Nankai Shitai*), built around the 55th Infantry Group and 144th Infantry drawn from the 55th Division. It was assembled in Korea in November, sent briefly to Japan and then departed for Chichi Jima in late November. The 5th Company, Maizuri 2d SNLF, based on Saipan, was to be the only unit to engage in combat during the invasion. The 4th Fleet would provide air support with the 22d Air Flotilla. The South Seas Detachment departed Chichi Jima on November 27 and put in at Haha Jima the next day. It was held there until departing for Guam on December 5.

South Seas Detachment (aka Horii Force) MajGen Horii Tomitaro (4,886)
HQ, 55th Infantry Group
144th Infantry Col Kusonose (2,925)
I Battalion, 55th Mountain Artillery
3d Company, 55th Cavalry (attached AT gun platoon)
1st Company, 55th Engineer
Company, 47th Field AA Battalion
Detachment, Medical Unit, 55th Division
Detachment, 1st Field Hospital, 55th Division
Detachment, Water Supply Unit, 55th Division
5th Company (+), Maizuri 2d SNLF 370

Only 153 Marines, 270 mostly unarmed Navy personnel, and a lightly armed militia of 300 defended Guam. There were no fortifications, heavy weapons, or aircraft. Air attacks struck Guam on 8 December immediately after the Pearl Harbor attack. In the early morning hours the SNLF company landed north of Agaña, the island's capital, with 144th Infantry battalions landing at points on the west, southwest, and east coats with all units converging on Agaña. After token resistance the defenders surrendered with light losses on both sides. The 4th Fleet was assigned responsibility for Guam, renamed Omiya Jima (Great Shrine Island), and elements of the Maizuru 2d SNLF took over occupation duties.

The South Seas Detachment departed Guam on January 14 to occupy Rabaul, New Britain, the R Operation. Rabaul and Kavieng, New Ireland and other towns on the islands and on New Guinea were first bombed on January 20. Some

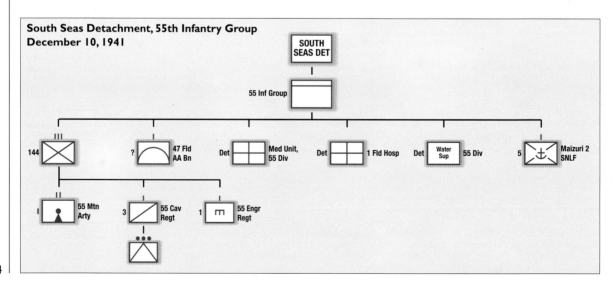

South Seas Detachment, 55th Infantry Group
December 10, 1941

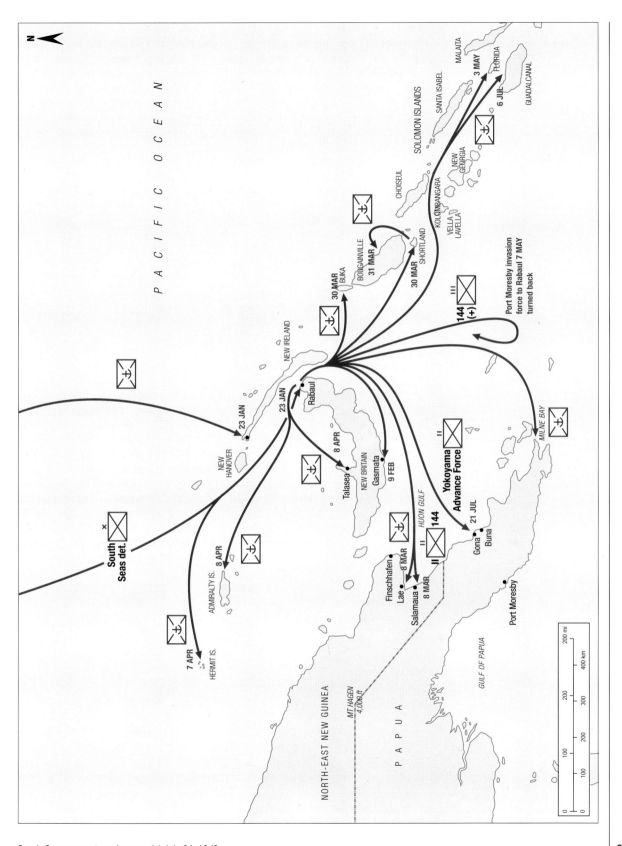

South Seas operations, January 14–July 21, 1942.

1,400 Australian toops without benefit of fortifications or combat aircraft defended Rabaul. No effort was made to reinforce or evacuate the garrison. The South Seas Detachment landed after midnight on the 23rd and routed the defenders by dawn. Most survivors headed for the north coast where about 400 were eventually evacuated. Two companies of the Maizuru 2d SNLF departed Truk on January 20 to occupy undefended Kavieng on the 23rd. SNLF elements occupied small towns on New Britain's south coast on February 9 and the north on April 8. The Admiralty Islands were occupied on the same date by SNLF troops from Rabaul. The 51st Transport Regiment served as an *ad hoc* occupation force.

Rabaul was developed as a major naval and air base on the island's northeast end and its neutralization became the focus of Allied operations in the South Pacific once a foothold was gained in the Solomons. Airfields and light defenses were established on New Ireland to protect the eastern approaches to New Britain. Rabaul became the headquarters for the newly organized 8th Fleet, which took over operations in the area, relieving the 4th Fleet.

The 23d Air Flotilla on Roi and Wotje Islands in the Marshalls commenced air attacks on Wake Island on December 8 lasting through the 19th. The 4th Fleet attempted a landing on the 11th, but was repulsed before 450 Maizuru 2d SNLF troops were debarked. Carrier attacks lasted from December 21 to 23 when 1,000 Maizuru 2d SNLF troops from Kwajalein landed on the south shores. The 450 Marine and 70 Navy defenders killed almost 400 of the landing force before capitulating.

The 4th Fleet was solely responsible for initial operations in the Gilberts and Solomons. The Gilbert Islands, part of the Gilbert and Ellice Crown Colony, were located only 300 miles to the southeast of the Japanese Marshalls. Other than a few coastwatchers there were no British military forces in the Gilberts and no airfields. The Japanese desired the Gilberts to deny the Allies bases within easy air range of the Marshalls and to serve as an out guard for the Mandate.

On December 8 a company of the 51st Guard Force (*51 Keibitai*) occupied Makin Island in Butartiari Atoll in the northern Gilberts. A small seaplane base and radio station was established. (Marines raided this facility in August 1942 with partial success. Makin and Tarawa were strengthened as a result.) The same unit then landed on Betio Island in Tarawa Atoll on the 10th. They rounded up a few Europeans and departed, but returned on the 24th and collected seven coastwatchers. Returning on September 3, 1942 they picked up another 17 coastwatchers and five other Europeans, who were murdered. The Yokosuka 6th SNLF occupied Tarawa in force at this time and placed a detachment on Makin.

Japanese forays into the Solomons did not commence until January 22, 1942 when the IJN bombed Tulagi, the Solomons' administrative center, as Rabaul was seized. On March 30–31 SNLF troops occupied Buka Island on the north end of Bougainville and Shortland Island on the south. This area would serve as an out guard for Rabaul and a staging area for future operations into the southern Solomons.

To provide a forward staging area to support operations on Papua and future operations further to the southeast, a detachment of the Kure 3d SNLF seized Tulagi and Gavutu on May 4. In mid-June the Japanese began construction of an airfield on Guadalcanal, which was discovered by the US in early July.

The June 4–5 Battle of Midway proved to be the turning point of the war with the loss of three carriers. The intended landing force was the 2d Combined Landing Force with 1,250 troops from the Yokosuka 5th SNLF and 1,200 troops of the Ichiki Force (28th Infantry [-], 7th Division) plus the IJN 11th and 12th Construction Units. The planned August operations to seize Fiji, New Caledonia, and Samoa were cancelled on July 11, 1942. The 9,000-man Kawaguchi Detachment was to occupy Fiji, the 5,500-man South Seas Detachment would seize New Caledonia, and a 1,200-man battalion of the Aboa Detachment would land on Samoa. These were backed by the Yazawa Force (see 17th Army below). In light of the Allied defense forces on those islands, these forces were inadequate. Japan conducted no further advances of significance after July 11, 1942.

New Guinea

The Japanese largely ignored Dutch New Guinea until April 1942 when small SNLF elements occupied a few sites on the north coast. Airfields and barge-staging bases were established to support operations in northeast New Guinea. A few small islands off the south and southwest coasts were also occupied.

The Japanese were more interested in the Huron Gulf area on the north coast of northeast New Guinea and the island's east end, Papua. Planning by the 4th Fleet had begun in February to secure the Huron Gulf area for airfields and its mineral resources. On March 8, II/144 Infantry of the South Seas Detachment landed at Salamaua while the Maizuru 2d SNLF seized Lea. On the 11th an SNLF element took Fischhafen. These units had staged out of Rabaul. II/144 was relieved by the 1,300-man 82d Guard Force to defend the area.

In April the 4th Fleet launched the MO Operation, an effort to seize Port Moresby on the south coast of Papua. The 144th Infantry, detached from the South Seas Detachment, and the Kure 3d SNLF departed Rabaul, but the attack convoy was intercepted by US carrier forces. The convoy, suffering severe losses, was turned back during the Battle of the Coral Sea lasting from May 4 to 8. This was Japan's first major defeat in the war.

On May 18 the 17th Army was activated at Davao, Mindanao to control IJA operations in the South Pacific. Under the command of LtGen Hyakutake Seikichi, its headquarters were moved to Rabaul on July 24 followed by its assigned units. When organized all assigned units were at Davao with the exception of the South Seas Detachment at Rabaul.

Unable to seize Port Moresby by sea, the Yokoyama Advance Force was landed at Gona on the north coast of Papua on July 22. A native track led from

17th Army
South Seas Detachment (55th Infantry Group with 144th Infantry)
Kawaguchi Detachment (35th Infantry Brigade with 124th Infantry)
Yazawa Force (41st Infantry, 55th Division)
Aoba Detachment (4th Infantry, 2d Division)*
15th Independent Engineer
*The remainder of the 2d Division was assigned on August 29 to make a second amphibious attempt to seize Port Moresby once the Kokodo Trail was secured. Cancelled in September.

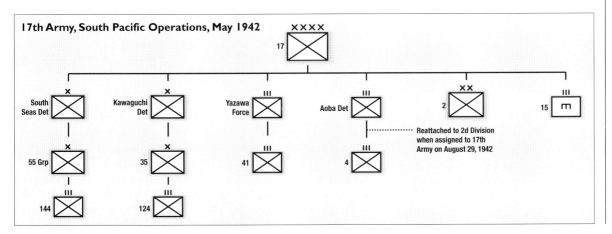

17th Army, South Pacific Operations, May 1942

nearby Buna over the Owen Stanley Mountains and the Japanese believed they could seize Port Moresby via an overland route à la Singapore, regardless of the 145-mile mud trail, at least half again as long because of elevation changes, crossed some of the most inhospitable terrain in the world. Optimistically, the Aboa Detachment had been formed on 18 May as a follow-on occupation force for Port Moresby and later Samoa.

Yokoyama **Advance** Force Col Yokoyama Yosuke
I Battalion, 144th Infantry 855
15th Independent Engineer 1,000
47th Field AA Battalion (- company) 265
Company, 55th Mountain Artillery 200
Service units
Laborers and porters 1,200 New Britain natives
Company (+), Sasebo 5th SNLF 300
15th Naval Construction Unit 800

Thus began the brutal seesaw battle for the Kokodo Trail lasting into September. The rest of the 144th Infantry was committed along with the South Seas Detachment HQ (aka Horii Detachment; 4,400 troops) and 41st Infantry (- I Battalion) (2,133 troops) under Col Yazawa Kiyomi. The Australians halted the advance with the Japanese 27 air miles from Port Moresby. The IGHQ ordered the 17th Army to halt the advance on August 29. From the end of the month the 17th Army was directed to concentrate on ejecting US forces from Guadalcanal. The units on the trail were ordered to withdraw and establish a defensive position in the Gona-Buna area on September 24. This would lead to an extremely ferocious battle lasting into January 1943.

One last offensive effort was conducted in late-August. The 8th Fleet sent a force to seize Milne Bay on the southeast end of Papua to provide a base to support the still-planned Port Moresby assault and operations on Guadalcanal. The 1,200-man Hayashi Force (1st Landing Force), launched from New Ireland, landed on the bay's north shore on the night of August 25. The 770-man Yano Force (2d Landing Force) came ashore on the 29th. The Australians defeated the mixed SNLF troops and the survivors were evacuated on September 4–5. The vicious battles for eastern New Guinea and the Solomons were only just beginning.

South Seas Detachment artillerymen man-pack a 7.5cm Type 94 (1934) mountain gun up the Kokoda Trail, Papua New Guinea. Horses were unable to withstand the rigors of the harsh climate and the steep, slippery track. The Japanese had thought that the first portion of the trail could accept truck traffic, but it turned out to be an indistinct mud footpath. (Uasburo Ihara)

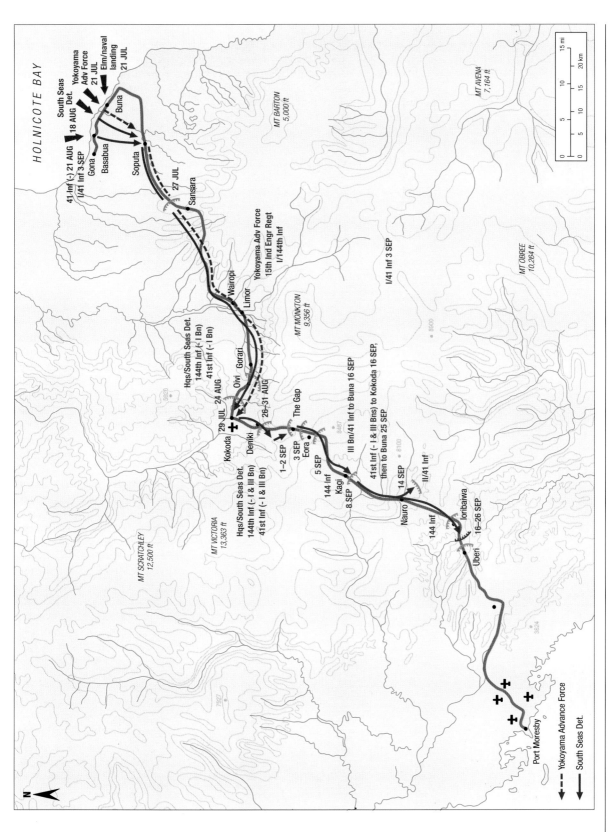

The battle for the Kokoda Trail, July 21–September 26, 1942. The Yokoyama Advance Force combined with the South Seas Detachment after reaching Kokoda.

Lessons learned

The Japanese learned a great deal in these early battles, but higher commands often failed to implement them Army-wide. At the unit level (division and below) the lessons learned in combat were absorbed, especially with regard to tactics, fire support, and field craft. Development of amphibious operations all but ceased as the Japanese moved on to the defensive in late-1942.

There were few organizational changes at any level. The most noticeable changes were the eventual elimination of the infantry group headquarters from most divisions and three rather than four rifle companies per battalion. The infantry group headquarters were often used to organize IMBs. A small number of divisions received a 10cm howitzer battalion in place of their third 7.5cm battalion. Because of shortages of 7cm battalion guns, due to their cost and the length of training required for them, some infantry gun units were equipped with the 8cm mortar, which was a more effective and portable weapon for jungle warfare. Few divisions retained four field hospitals with most being reduced to three or even two. Most divisions converted their cavalry regiments to reconnaissance, though they may have retained the cavalry designation. Many new divisions lacked either. The last of the square divisions were triangularized by reassigning an infantry regiment and a brigade HQ, and the internal reorganization of divisional units adjusted. Increased numbers of AA units were raised, as were artillery and engineer units. Additional shipping engineer and other units to support waterborne operations in the South Seas were also activated. The tank group was eliminated in 1942, being insufficient to control tactical operations. Additional tank regiments were raised and three small tank divisions were organized in Manchuria in 1942.

Surprisingly, only eight infantry divisions were activated in early-1942, largely from existing IMBs and independent regiments. A large number of IMBs and garrison units were raised though to secure occupied territories. It would not be until the summer of 1943 that ten additional divisions were raised. The IJA Air Service was greatly expanded and reorganized with the former air groups becoming air armies. The vast area Japan now controlled and its widely dispersed units required the activation of additional army and area army headquarters to allow effective command and control, as well as logistical support.

With the rush to produce equipment, munitions, and all types of logistical *matériel*, there was little time for quality control, integration of improvements, and improved packaging. Some effort was made to improve munitions packaging to protect them from the climate extremes of the tropics. A great deal of ammunition and related items deteriorated and malfunctioned because of the poor weatherproofing of their packaging.

Very few new weapons were introduced during the war. New infantry weapons did appear in 1942: a lighter 7.7mm HMG, the improved 4.7cm AT gun, and a 12cm mortar, to name a few. Japanese research and development had largely stagnated before the war. Material resources, manufacturing capabilities, and time constraints forced Japan to retain the tried and proven weapons already in use, even though many were inadequate. Even with new development efforts it would have taken up to two years for any new weapons to be developed and produced in quantity. Japan could ill-afford downtime as factories were retooled for new weapons. The fabrication of existing weapons was increased, but production could not keep up with the demands of equipping new units and replacing combat losses. Because of *matériel* shortages, much that was available was committed to aircraft and ship production.

Chronology

1939

February	Japan occupies Hainan Island off the South China coast.
May	Japan initiates a long-running offensive against Soviet forces on the Manchuria–Siberia border, but is defeated in September.

1940

July	Due to reverses in China, Japan mobilizes 1,000,000 men.
2 July	The US enacts export control law restricting the supply of fuel and other war materials to Japan.
21 July	Japan pressurizes the government of Indochina to accept Japanese occupation after the fall of France.
25 September	Japanese forces occupy Hanoi in Indochina.
27 September	Japan forms the Tripartite Military Alliance with Germany and Italy.

1941

13 April	The Japanese–Soviet Non-Aggression Pact is concluded.
27 May	The US President declares a state of "full emergency," authorizing armed forces to readiness levels to repel a threat in the Western Hemisphere.
26 July	The US freezes Japanese assets.
5 November	Japan commits to war with the Western Powers.
6 November	The Southern Army is activated and units assigned.
27–28 November	4th US Marines depart China for the Philippines.
2 December	"X-Day" is set for the commencement of hostilities.
7 December	Japan attacks Malaya, Pearl Harbor, and the Philippines.
10 December	Japan assaults Guam, and US forces surrender there. Japanese land on northern Luzon. HMS *Prince of Wales* and HMS *Repulse* are sunk.
12 December	Japanese forces land on southeast Luzon.
14 December	Thailand declares an alliance with Japan.
16 December	The Japanese land in British Borneo.
20 December	Japanese forces land on Mindanao.
22 December	Japanese forces land in Ligayen Gulf, Luzon.
23 December	Japan assaults Wake Island, and US forces surrender.
24 December	A second Japanese landing on southeast Luzon takes place.
25 December	Hong Kong falls to Japanese forces.

1942

2 January	Manila, capital of the Philippines, falls.
11 January	Japanese troops land on Dutch Borneo (Tarakan Island) and Celebes.
15 January	Japanese forces cross into Burma from Thailand.
23 January	Japanese troops land on New Britain and seize Rabaul.
8 February	Japanese forces suspend offensive operations on Bataan.
14 February	Japanese forces land on southern Sumatra.
15 February	The fall of Singapore.
19 February	Japanese forces land on Bali.
20 February	Japanese forces land on Dutch and Portuguese Timor.
26 February	Japanese forces land on Mindoro.

1 March	Japanese troops land on West and East Java.
12 March	Japanese forces land on northern Sumatra.
12 March	The Japanese resume the Bataan offensive after reinforcement.
8 April	Japanese troops land in the Admiralty Islands.
9 April	US–Filipino forces surrender on the Bataan Peninsula.
10 April	Japanese forces land on Cebu.
16 April	Japanese troops land on Panay.
24 April	The Doolittle raid is conducted on Tokyo.
4–8 May	The Battle of the Coral Sea. The Japanese Port Moresby invasion force withdraws.
5–6 May	Japanese assault Corregidor, and US–Filipino forces surrender.
20 May	Commonwealth forces withdraw from Burma into India.
Spring	Japan activates eight new infantry divisions.
4–5 June	The Battle for Midway.
13–21 June	Japan seizes Attu and Kiska, Aleutian Islands.
9 June	Last US–Filipino forces surrender in the Philippines.
11 July	Japan cancels the invasions of Fiji, New Caledonia, and Samoa.
22 July	Japanese forces land at Buna-Gona and attempt to seize Port Moresby from inland. The Battle for the Kokodo Trail continues until September.
7 August	US Marines assault Guadalcanal-Tulagi.
24 September	The Japanese defense of Buna-Gona begins.

Bibliography

Cook, Taya and Theodore F. *Japan at War: An Oral History* (New York, NY, The New Press, 1992)

Daugherty, Leo J., III *Fighting Techniques of a Japanese Infantryman, 1941–1945: Training, Techniques, and Weapons* (St Paul, MN, MBI Publishing, 2002)

Drea, Edward J. *In the Service of the Emperor: Essays on the Imperial Japanese Army* (Lincoln, NA, University of Nebraska Press, 1998)

Forty, George *Japanese Army Handbook, 1939–1945* (Stroud, UK, Sutton Publishing, 1999)

Fuller, Richard *Shokan—Hirohito's Samurai: Leaders of the Japanese Armed Forces 1926–1945* (London, UK, Arms and Armour Press, 1992)

Harris, Meirion and Susie *Soldiers of the Sun: the Rise and Fall of the Imperial Japanese Army* (New York, NY, Random House, 1991)

Hayashi, Saburo and Coox, Alvin D. *Kogun: The Japanese Army in the Pacific War* (Quantico, VA, Marine Corps Association, 1959). Published in Japan in 1951 as *Taiheiyo Senso Rikusen Gaishi.*

Henshall, Kenneth G. *A History of Japan: from Stone Age to Superpower* (New York, NY, St Martin's Press, 1999)

Hough, LtCol Frank O.; Ludwig, Maj Verle E.; and Shaw, Henry I. Jr. *History of US Marine Corps Operations in World War II. Vol. I: Pearl Harbor to Guadalcanal* (Washington, DC, US Government Printing Office, 1958)

Humphreys, Leonard A. *The Way of the Heavenly Sword: the Japanese Army in the 1920s* (Stanford, CA, 1995)

Ienaga, Saburo *The Pacific War, 1931–1945: a Critical Perspective of Japan's Role in World War II* (New York, NY, Random House, 1978)

Long, Gavin M. *The Six Years War: a Concise History of Australia in the 1939–1945 War* (Canberra, Australia, The Australian War Memorial and the Australian Government Publishing Service, 1973)

Morison, Samuel E. *History of US Navy Operations in World War II. Vol. III: the Rising Sun in the Pacific, 1931–April 1942* (Boston, MA, Little Brown and Co., 1948)

Morton, Louis *United States Army in World War II: the Fall of the Philippines* (Washington, DC, US Government Printing Office, 1953)

Rottman, Gordon L. *US Marine Corps Order of Battle: Ground and Air Units in the Pacific War, 1939–1945* (Westport, CT, Greenwood Publishing, 2002)

Rottman, Gordon L. *World War II Pacific Island Guide: a Geo-Military Study* (Westport, CT, Greenwood Publishing, 2002)

Toland, John *The Rising Sun: the Decline and Fall of the Japanese Empire, 1939–1945* (New York, NY, Random House, 1970)

War Department, *Handbook on Japanese Military Forces*, TM-E 30-480, September 15, 1944 with Change 3, June 1, 1945.

Whitman, John W. *Bataan: Our Last Ditch* (New York, NY, Hippocrene Books, 1990)

Abbreviations and linear measurements

AAA	antiaircraft artillery		LMG	light machine gun
ABDACOM	American-British-Dutch-Australian Command		NAS	Navy Air Service
APHE	Armor-piercing high explosive		NCO	non-commissioned officer
AT	antitank		NEI	Netherlands East Indies
Bn	Battalion		Regt	Regiment
Btry	Battery		SNLF	Special Naval Landing Force(s)
Co	Company			
CO	commanding officer		**Officer ranks**	
CP	command post		Lt	Lieutenant
Det	Detachment		1stLt	1st Lieutenant
FA	Field artillery		2dLt	2d Lieutenant
HE	High explosive		Capt	Captain
HMG	heavy machine gun		Maj	Major
HQ	Headquarters		LtCol	Lieutenant-Colonel
IGHQ	Imperial General Headquarters		Col	Colonel
IIB	Independent Infantry Battalion		BGen	Brigadier-General
IJA	Imperial Japanese Army		MajGen	Major-General
IJN	Imperial Japanese Navy		LtGen	Lieutenant-General
IMB	Independent Mixed Brigade			

Distances, ranges, and dimensions are given in the contemporary US system of inches, feet, yards, and statute miles rather than metric:

feet to meters:	multiply feet by 0.3048
yards to meters:	multiply yards by 0.9144
miles to kilometers:	multiply miles by 1.6093

Weapon calibers are given in the standard Japanese metric system:

centimeters to inches	multiply by 0.3937

Index

References to illustrations are shown in **bold**.